Enter Every Trembling Heart

Enter Every Trembling Heart

Prayers for Christian Worship

John Killinger

Abingdon Press

Nashville

ENTER EVERY TREMBLING HEART
PRAYERS FOR CHRISTIAN WORSHIP

Copyright © 2003 by Abingdon Press

This book is printed on acid-free paper.

Library of Congress Cataloging-in-Publication Data

Killinger, John.
    Enter every trembling heart : prayers for Christian worship / John Killinger.
        p. cm.
    ISBN 0-687-09395-3 (pbk. : alk. paper)
    1. Pastoral prayers. I. Title.

BV250 .K55 2003
264'.13—dc21

2002152776

03 04 05 06 07 08 09 10 11 12—10 9 8 7 6 5 4 3 2 1
MANUFACTURED IN THE UNITED STATES OF AMERICA

*This book is joyfully dedicated to my dear friend
THOMAS SOMERVILLE,
who was for many years Minister of Music at the
great First Congregational Church of Los Angeles,
where many of these prayers were offered, and
whose relentless search for dignity and perfection
in worship doubtless contributed to their quality,
if such they have; and to his lovely wife,
VIRGINIA SOMERVILLE,
who was my invaluable colleague and secretary
during my all-too-brief ministry there, and whose
inimically melodic voice and spirit will always
remind me of a thousand glockenspiels on parade!*

Contents

Introduction

The prayers and affirmations in this book, as in its pred-ecessor *Lost in Wonder, Love, and Praise,* were first composed for public worship in three very different congregations: the First Presbyterian Church of Lynchburg, Virginia, the First Congregational Church of Los Angeles, and the Little Stone Church on Mackinac Island, Michigan. I have been forcibly struck, in revising them for publication, by how frequently certain themes echo through their pages and how accurate-ly, as a whole, these represent the core of my personal theology.

Among these themes are *the joy of truly seeing the world around us; the responsibility of those who have food, money, edu-cation, or technology for those who don't have them; the wonder and beauty of being servants; the offensiveness to God of insensi-tivity, arrogance, or false piety; the importance of being open to people whose backgrounds and ideologies differ from our own; and above all, the mystical and incomprehensible, yet loving and com-passionate nature of God.*

Some of these themes, I now realize, may well have been offensive to certain members of my congregations, for they emphasize, both in individual prayers and collectively, the intractability of holiness—what my friend Martin Bell calls the *up-against-it-ness* of God—whereby we are reminded, whenever we come within even the remote vicinity of tran-scendence, that God doesn't dance to our tunes, and, in fact, doesn't approve of some of them. Yet I cannot remember a single instance, in any of my congregations, when even the most outspoken or umbrageous member reproached me for something uttered in a prayer.

I was not so lucky, I confess, with my sermons. But there was something about the prayers—possibly the fact that they were addressed to God and not to the congregation—that exempted them from the realm of ordinary discourse and therefore permitted in them a surprisingly frequent repetition of the most radical ideas of our faith. For this reason, I think prayer must be one of the most truly subversive elements of Christian worship. It is the part of the liturgy where we come closest to shaping or reshaping the ideology of our congregations without having to stand in the dock for doing so.

I was particularly struck, in rereading the prayers, by their frequent mention of the words *broken* and *brokenness*, as though this somehow were the bottom line of the human condition I was describing. There were countless references also to the poor, the hungry, the ill, the neglected, the lonely, the disaffected, and the disenfranchised. But *fragmentation* and *brokenness* seemed to preside as the overall description of the situation out of which both individual worshipers and the Christian community as a whole offer their prayers to God.

We *are* broken. Everything from the daily newspaper and TV reports to our frankest confessions of our personal situations attests to that. We *have been* broken, we *are* broken, and we *shall be* broken. Only God offers wholeness and togetherness, and that is what forms the dialectic of all praying: We, out of the fractured, myopic, and wayward state of our humanity, come before God, who is perfectly unified, righteous, and caring, to seek what we so desperately need, namely, forgiveness and reconciliation with the transcendent, eternal Deity.

If there is anything "prophetic" about these prayers, it arises from the juxtaposition of *our brokenness* and *God's wholeness*. God has shown us what is good: to do justice, to love mercy, and to walk humbly before the Divine Being. And when we come before the Deity with anything approximating a true realization of the audacity of such an act, we are instantly confronted with our pitiful inadequacy, and, indeed, the inadequacy of any human institution, even—or *especially*—the church. Our first instinct then is that of Isaiah, to fall on our faces and cry, "O woe is me, for I am unclean, and I dwell in the midst of an unclean people!"* And our next, when we realize we have not been struck dead by the Deity, is to bargain, to ask for what we need, and our society needs, to become more like the Deity: to be more aware of everything, more unified, more caring. That, we know, is what is required for our redemption. And in the presence of the Deity there is nothing we want more than to be redeemed, to become part of the transcendent Mystery of the universe.

This is why the words *rule, reign,* and *kingdom* appear so frequently in the prayers. Jesus said we are to pray for God's kingdom to come among us. God's rule or kingdom is a metaphor for the universal will of the Deity, whereby all things are kept in harmony with the Deity and thus exist in their truest and fullest dimensions.

This kingdom, which occupies so much of Jesus' teaching in all of the Gospels, will not be completely realized until the *eschaton,* or end of all things, as described in the book of Revelation. But Jesus discerned it as *presently existing among us,* for those who have eyes to see and ears to hear; it is *already* on its way, like a phantom whose form will soon totally materialize. When we pray, therefore, we have to remain acutely aware of the kingdom and its demands on us. Otherwise, our praying would be less than Christian, for its concerns and petitions would be framed without regard for our Master's most central preoccupation.

Brokenness, wholeness, kingdom—these are important elements in prayer. They don't limit prayer, but they do help define it. They remind us that prayer, at its most faithful, is not mere meditation or waiting before the divine presence.

* Isaiah 6:5, author's paraphrase.

On the contrary, it has a specific theological content that keeps being repeated over and over so that it teaches as it heals and inclines the mind while unifying the soul. This content is the core of Jesus' own teachings about life, death, love, fellowship, service, sacrifice, and everything else about which he spoke. Perhaps this is why he said we should pray in his name—because we can honestly and without hesitance affix his name to any prayer that is molded around his view of the world and how we should live in it. It doesn't deny other forms of prayer as practiced by Muslims, Buddhists, Sikhs, or Hindus. It merely *is* as one form of prayer that we have found effective in addressing the Deity and shaping our own religious consciousness. That is to say, it works for us, and we are bound in the end to thank God for it.

Which reminds me—there is also a great deal of thanksgiving in these prayers and affirmations. David Steindl-Rast says that gratitude is the very heart of prayer, implying that until we have reached a state of voluntary and joyous thankfulness we probably have not really learned how to address the Deity at all. There is much validity in this. The truer our perspective on both God and ourselves, the more we realize how gracious God is, and how completely we are and have always been at the mercy of the Deity. And this realization greatly colors our understanding of our selves and our role in the world, so that, in turn, it radically modifies the object of our praying.

When we are truly thankful, as we ought to be, we shall not wish to utter a single petition for ourselves. For others, yes, but not for ourselves, because we shall see ourselves as already blessed beyond all reason and understanding—even beyond all imagining. This is surely why Jesus omitted all personal or physical requests from the model prayer except the one for daily bread; anything more would be superfluous and out of character for those whose one master desire has become the kingdom of God.

Lest this all sound too knowing and authoritative, let me conclude by recalling how embarrassingly flimsy and inadequate all our prayers are, and how incapable of securing the intimate bond between Deity and subject that must surely be the object of true devotion. "Lord, teach us to pray" is a cry that ought to be on all our lips, for there is obviously nothing more important for any of us than knowing how to live in the presence of God, and yet nothing at which most of us, because of our sheer, implacable humanity, are more clumsy and inept.

If the prayers and affirmations in this book are helpful— if in any way they point you to a kind of praying and being-in-the-world that whets your appetite for more substantial forms of prayer and devotion—then I am very happy. But one of the worst things you could do is to take them as anything more than models for your own praying or awkwardly erected signposts pointing the way to the work you yourself must do, in struggling with language and ideas and a sense of the Divine Mystery, to produce the prayers of your own heart.

We need never fear, in this life, that we shall find ourselves unable to go farther in prayer. There will always be a mountain beyond the one we have climbed, a trackless plain beyond the one just traversed, inviting us forward and promising greater rewards if we will but prepare ourselves for fresh and ever more difficult explorations. But I can promise you now, although I am sure you already know it, that there is absolutely nothing in the entire field of human endeavors more ultimately satisfying, even when it frustrates or disappoints us, than the effort to communicate with God!

ONE

Calls to Worship

1

Leader: Today is the day the Lord has made.
People: **It is a day for singing and worship.**
Leader: God is with us in our celebration.
People: **Let us sing and worship with all our hearts!**

2

The mysterious air of this place summons us away from a world of war and deceit, crime and distrust, into a world of peace and truth, wholeness and joy, where God is all in all, and we learn to live in that world by being in the divine presence. Even better, we learn to make the other world God's world and to become agents of transformation and change, sharing the divine love and peace with even those who consider themselves our enemies. Let us worship God!

3

The chimes call us to another dimension of our own reality, from the world of work and leisure, travel and responsibility, holiday and home, to a world of spirit, of prayer and the inner self, of transcendence and holiness. It is not always easy to enter this new dimension, or to remain there with concentration when we have accomplished the entrance. But it is always worth it, for it returns us to the former dimension with new hope and vision and centeredness. It reminds us that God cares about all our dimensions and is in all our worlds. Let us worship God in prayer and thoughtfulness.

4

Leader: O God, we want to be more than happy; we want to be joyful.

People: **O God, we want to be more than healthy; we want to be whole.**

Leader: O God, we want to be more than alive; we want to be radiant.

People: **O God, we want to be more than adequate; we want to be triumphant.**

Leader: With all these hopes and intentions before us, let us worship God.

5

Leader: God has made a wonderful world.

People: **Let us live in the world with joy!**

Leader: God has made us companions of the Divine Spirit.

People: **Let us praise God with all our hearts!**

6

Leader: "O come, let us sing to the LORD;

People: **"Let us make a joyful noise to the rock of our salvation!**

Leader: "Let us come into his presence with thanksgiving;

People: **"Let us make a joyful noise to him with songs of praise!"***

7

Praise God for dappled things, said the poet Gerard Manley Hopkins: for cloudy skies, brindled cows, speckled trout, turning leaves, tie-dyed jeans, and even lives that have been mottled by sin. There is almost nothing for which we

---

* Psalm 95:1-2.

cannot praise God, if we only have eyes to see and ears to hear. Therefore let us worship and bow down. Let us open our hearts, and let us sing. Let us find joy in the act of praise!

8

The nights are cool now. There is a tinge of fall on the fields and trees. Many of our parishioners, like the geese, have begun to make their way southward for the winter. We are mindful of passing time and the seasons of life and a sense of our certain mortality. It is a good time for worshiping God, who presides over all times, all seasons, and even our mortality.

9

Leader: Happy are the people who have learned to worship God.
People: **Happy are those who walk in the divine presence.**
Leader: In God's name they shall rejoice all the day.
People: **God's righteousness shall bear them up forever.**
Leader: Let us worship and rejoice!

10

Leader: This is God's day, and we are God's people.
People: **Let us come into God's house with thanksgiving.**
Leader: Let us lift up our hearts with gladness.
People: **Let us sing praises to God's name forever and ever.**

11

There is a hush about holiness: A veil of quietness falls across our souls as we contemplate the presence of God in human affairs and realize that the hand that shaped the vastness of the cosmos is also working out our eternal destiny. Therefore we perform little rituals of recognition, such as kneeling or bowing our heads, lowering our voices, crossing ourselves, and reciting ancient creeds and prayers, hoping thereby to re-create the mood of reception in which others in other places and times have experienced a divine visitation. We seek an inner meeting, a transformation, a moment of blessing that will hallow and direct our future lives. We dare to approach the center of holiness. Let us therefore be in prayer and worship God.

12

Leader: "I was glad when they said to me, 'Let us go to the house of the LORD!'"*

People: **There is a feeling of life and wholeness here that we need for living.**

Leader: There is a sense of Christ's presence here that renews our spirits.

People: **Let us rejoice in his presence and sing the glories of his name!**

13

Leader: This is one of the days the Lord has made.

People: **Let us rejoice and be glad in it!**

Leader: God has called us to be a special people and to witness to the presence of Christ.

People: **Let us praise and glorify God's name!**

14

A Call to Worship for Advent

Leader: The baby who was born in Bethlehem is alive today.

People: **Come, Lord Jesus!**

---

* Psalm 122:1.

18

Leader:	Death has no power over him; he walks the world as our risen Lord.
People:	**Come, Lord Jesus!**
Leader:	We can feel his presence now as we sing and pray and hear the Word.
People:	**Come, Lord Jesus!**

15
A Call to Worship for Christmas

Leader:	It is a time of angels and shepherds and wise men.
People:	**The world has turned to Bethlehem once more.**
Leader:	We bring praises and gifts to the one born in a manger.
People:	**O come, let us adore him!**

16

Leader:	"In the beginning was the Word"*—
People:	**The wonderful, indescribable Word!**
Leader:	And the Word became flesh in the man Jesus,
People:	**Who bore our sins on the tree.**
Leader:	He was raised in glory and freedom.
People:	**Let us praise his name in song and prayer!**

17

Leader:	This is the gathering.
People:	**From time immemorial, people have gathered to honor God.**
Leader:	They have gathered to be caught up in the Spirit of God.
People:	**They have gathered—*we* have gathered—to worship the Lord our God.**
Leader:	There is nothing we ever do that is more important.

---

* John 1:1.

People: **Then let us join our hearts and souls in singing to God!**

18

Leader: This is the beautiful day the Lord has made!

People: **It is a day for singing and praying and loving one another.**

Leader: It is a day for assessing our lives and our attitudes,

People: **And for considering the possibility that they could both be changed!**

Leader: Then let us worship the Lord our God!

19

Our beautiful prelude calls us away from a world of war and crime and deceit into a world of prayer and meditation, where God is known in the inner spirit and our lives are renewed for daily existence. By entering this second world we are able to carry redemption back into the first one and help to renew it as well for another week. What we are doing here is, therefore, very important. Let us worship God.

20

The dwelling of God is among us, says the Bible, and the love of the divine has entered our midst and changed us forever. Once more, our doors are open to proclaim the presence of love and forgiveness and to welcome all who join us under this pleasant umbrella of grace. Let us luxuriate in a spirit of worship!

21

The beautiful tones of the organ call us once more to a time of praise and meditation, of reverence and revelation, as we pause before the Maker of everything that is. It is so easy to rush through our days without seeing the deeper relationships among things, and especially our own deeper relationship to God. Therefore a time like this is a special treasure. Let us value it by truly worshiping God.

22

Leader:	Every day is beautiful where God is,
People:	**And every fellowship is warm.**
Leader:	Every wound is healed
People:	**And every soul is healthy.**
Leader:	Every prospect is wonderful
People:	**And every future is assured.**
Leader:	Let us worship God!

23

"When the earth totters, with all its inhabitants," says God in the Psalms, "it is I who keep its pillars steady."* There is something steady about this place, isn't there? About being in church on Sunday morning and feeling the presence of the One who keeps the pillars from rocking. Let us sing praises to the eternal God!

24

Leader:	In the summer, we see God in leafy trees and beautiful gardens.
People:	**In the fall, we see God in the clear, blue skies and nature's patchwork of glorious colors.**
Leader:	In the winter, we see God in the sternness of the frozen earth and patterns of frost on our windowpanes.
People:	**In the spring, we see God in the thawing lakes and swelling buds.**
All:	**In fact, there is no time when we cannot see God or feel God in the resonance of our bodies to the glory of God's creation.**

* Psalm 75:3.

Leader: It is Sunday morning.

People: **Let us praise God with our songs and our prayers!**

25

What is more changeable than the weather, unless it is life itself? And yet, in the midst of all the change, there is one Rock, one Hope, one stable, eternal Presence, and that is God. We are here to center our hearts and minds on God. Let us approach the Divine in worship!

26

Leader: "The mighty one, God the LORD," says the psalmist, "speaks and summons the earth from the rising of the sun to its setting. Out of Zion, the perfection of beauty, God shines forth."*

People: **And God shines forth out of the heavenly kingdom here, where God's people gather to sing his praises.**

Leader: Let us worship God!

27

Leader: On the golden days of sunshine or the silvery days of clouds and rain,

People: **God is always our bright and shining hope.**

Leader: God is the one who fills our hearts with love and joy.

People: **God helps us to become renewed and recentered for the best living of all our days.**

Leader: Therefore let us worship God.

---

* Psalm 50:1-2.

TWO

Opening Prayers

1

God of the winter cold and God of the summer heat,
God of the spring rains and God of the dry fields,
We worship you.
Yours is the earth in all its fullness,
And yours are our lives with all their complications.
Tune our hearts to sing your songs,
Lift our eyes to see your visions,
And give us voices to praise you.
Through Jesus Christ, who taught us to say,
Our Father. . . .

2

In the beauty and stillness of this sanctuary, O God, it is
easy to feel your presence and seek your will in our lives.
What is more difficult is to feel your presence and seek your
will in our ordinary lives, where we work and live under
stress and often fail in our resolutions. Help us while we are
here so to center our lives and hopes in you that the two
worlds may be brought together and we may carry the
sense of holiness and inspiration wherever we go, in the
name of Jesus of Nazareth, who taught us to pray, saying,
Our Father. . . .

3

We are here with many kinds of needs and expectations,
O God; let the shadow of your wings fall across us, that we

may know, deeply and intuitively, that we are in your presence. Then our wounds will be healed and our discomforts made bearable, our night will turn to day and our darkness to indescribable light. Then our hearts will sing again; and we shall face our lives with new hope and understanding; and love will blossom once more in the desert places of our hearts. Come, Lord Jesus, and lift our vision to the one you saw, of a world fitly joined together in your heavenly Father. Come, Holy Spirit, and make us one in service and dedication, as we pray together the prayer we have been taught to say, *Our Father. . . .*

4

Alleluia, O God, we praise your name for life and love and joy; for the bright and colorful world through which we passed to come here; for the history of service and sacrifice that adorns this church; for the hymns of poets and the songs of psalmists; for the confederation of friends and members and visitors who constitute this congregation; for the dream of the early Christians that is being fulfilled even now in our lives; and for the holy presence that settles on us as we pray, reminding us of an eternal life intermingling with the life we live now, comforting us, and encouraging us in this vale of suffering and mortality. Grant that we may now surrender all our cares and anxieties and be gathered up in the hope and confidence of your Holy Spirit, through Jesus Christ our Lord, who taught us to pray, saying, *Our Father. . . .*

5

O God of the early morning, when there is a nip in the air and the blackbirds talk to each other from the tall pine trees, we praise your name in song and prayer and sermon. Consecrate this day, with all its special meaning, to the service of your kingdom. Help us to lift our hearts and voices to make it ring with joy and purpose, and to set the tone for our lives throughout the coming week, when we shall take you into the market places and schools and travel terminals, and witness to our faith by our behavior to all the colleagues and teachers and students and neighbors and clerks and others we find there. In the name of Jesus, our Lord. Amen.

6

O God, giver of life and truth and grace, we gather today in a spirit of thanksgiving for all your mercies. We praise your name for your faithfulness to your people through the ages, and for the gift of your son, Jesus, in whom we have remission of our sin and renewal of our hearts. Receive each one of us as we come before you in humility and supplication, through Christ our Lord, who taught us to pray, saying, *Our Father*....

7

O God who has made the heavens and the earth, who has surrounded us with beauty and goodness, help us to see what you have made and to fall down before you in wonder. Let our hearts open before you like the flowers of the field, and praise you for the sun and the morning. For you are the giver of every perfect gift, and have given us your son Jesus Christ, who taught us to pray, saying, *Our Father. . . .*

8

O God, whom no one has ever seen but whose love and generosity are always visible in the best of human relationships and in the beauty and serenity of our own homes, we praise you for your faithfulness through all generations and worship you now in song and prayer and gift. Bestow a blessing upon each one who has come today, and especially upon our guests, that we may see our lives and affairs more clearly, love one another more dearly, and give ourselves more unstintingly to you and the world around us, through Jesus Christ our Lord. Amen.

9

O God, whose glory is seen in dappled skies and evening sunsets and whose care is known in a mother's love or a father's tenderness, we praise you for your continuing goodness to us, which has brought us safely through another week in health and strength and abiding courage. We seek your face today in order to remember your steadfast care, find encouragement in righteousness, and discover the gifts with which you have so abundantly blessed us. Grant that in this time of sharing we may find forgiveness for our sins and renewed hope and inspiration for living in a flawed and sometimes difficult world. Through Jesus Christ our Lord. Amen.

10

Lord God of hosts, who spoke to us in ancient times through the law and the prophets, and who visited us in Jesus Christ, come now and make your presence known in our midst through song and prayer and sermon. Remind us of our salvation, grant us mercy for all our sin, and renew your spirit within us that we may rightly praise you and afterward serve you. Through Jesus Christ our Lord, who has taught us to pray, saying, *Our Father. . . .*

11

In the glory and beauty of this season, O God, we turn to you as the source of all glory and beauty and power. We may have come here for many reasons, but now we realize that you are the real reason, the one behind our comings and goings. You are the One who pulls and draws us, who has ordained before we were born that we should worship you this day. Prepare our hearts for hearing your word of confrontation and comfort, for approaching you in prayer and submission, for reaching out to one another in love and forgiveness, and for going out to serve those who dwell in hunger and poverty in the world beyond. Draw us now inward and downward toward the center of ourselves, where we may know ourselves and meet your transforming Spirit. In the name of Jesus Christ, who taught us to pray, saying, *Our Father*. . . .

12

O God of sights and sounds and truth and feelings, we praise you for the warmth of friendly greetings, the beauty of church music, the smells and colors of the season, the patterns of light and shadow on our lawns and streets, the energy pulsing in our bodies, the sense of worship in a place like this. Receive us now, rich in things but poor in soul. Set us on your knee like little children. Hear the humble prayers we make and the songs we sing. Teach us to seek your face, and renew us for life in your beautiful world. Through Jesus Christ our Lord, who taught us to pray, saying, *Our Father*. . . .

13

In the beauty and variety of this pleasant place, O God, we are reminded of your infinite creativity and generosity. You have lavished upon us outward loveliness and inward peace. You have filled us with a spirit of love and fellowship, and provided an agreeable house for our worship. You have given us the strength and agility to be here. Our cups overflow, and we have a feeling that goodness and mercy will follow us all the days of our lives. We thank you and praise you, in the name of our Lord Jesus, who taught us to pray, saying, *Our Father*. . . .

14

This is a day unlike any other that has ever been, O God, filled with the promise of flowers that have never before bloomed, thoughts that have never been thought, friends that have never been met, prayers that have never been uttered. Grant that we shall not miss it, but shall be alert in all our being to the wonder of it. Fill our hearts with praise and our spirits with exuberance. Help us to stand on tiptoe to meet your coming into our lives, for you are the loving Creator of everything, and your angels hover over us with bright healing in their wings. Through Jesus Christ our Lord. Amen.

15

Glory, laud, and honor be always yours, O God, for the amplitude of your creation, for the grace and mercy you have shown to us, and for the way you continue to refresh us in the troublesome parts of our journeys. We cannot imagine life without some knowledge of you to deepen its meaning and purpose. We come now with thanksgiving for the miracle of our very existence, and for the mystery of our faith that enables us to see what a miracle it is. Grant that our experience here today may be one of renewal and recommitment, both to you and to the values that have been instilled in us through Jesus Christ, our ever-present Lord, who teaches us to pray, saying, *Our Father.* . . .

16

We praise you, O God of the ages and Lord of all creation, and ask for your blessing, not only upon us but upon all the world. Grant that this day there may be an increase of love and tolerance in the world and a sense of understanding among its inhabitants. Break down the barriers of hate and prejudice, and help us to live with healing and forgiveness and acceptance. To that end, enable us to pray with true sincerity the prayer Jesus taught us, saying, *Our Father.* . . .

17

Ours is the sunlight, ours is the morning!* What a glorious promise, O God, what a wonderful hope! We praise you for

---

* Adapted from the hymn "Morning Has Broken" by Eleanor Farjeon. *The United Methodist Hymnal* (Nashville: The United Methodist Publishing House, 1989), no. 145.

the great mythic images of our faith that sustain us in the darkest, most trying moments of our pilgrimage. Teach us, in these difficult days, to spend more and more time recalling them, reliving them, feeding on them. Let them be for us, as for our fathers and mothers in the faith, great living truths that shape and reorder our existence, until we are fit to be yours forever, through Christ our Lord, who taught us to pray, saying, *Our Father....*

18

O God, who made the heavens and the earth, who has surrounded us with beauty and goodness, so that our hearts are lifted up at the sight of a little child in a baptismal dress or a field of flowers rising toward the sky, help us to see what you have made and to fall down before you in wonder and worship. Let our faith be like that of the child, and let our hearts open before you like the flowers of the field, that we may praise you for the sun and the morning. For you are the giver of every good and perfect gift and have given us your Son, Jesus Christ, who taught us to pray, saying, *Our Father....*

19

Holy, holy, holy, Lord God of hosts. The world praises you, O God. The sun, the stars, and the moon praise you. The mountains and the seas praise you. The meadows and rivers praise you. The grass and the trees and the sky praise you. The birds and the fish and the animals praise you. Now let us, who above all created beings were made to worship and adore you, praise you through Jesus Christ our Lord, who taught us to pray, saying, *Our Father....*

20

We praise you, O God, for the week that has passed and for the many gifts it has brought: for sunshine and cloud, openness and shelter, sights to delight the eye and thoughts to challenge the mind, friends and family to love and to cherish, work to stretch and sustain us, and now worship to repair our fellowship with you. Enfold us all, young and old, male and female, strong and weak, in the gentle comfort of your sustaining presence, and let us cherish the fact that none of us is alone, nor ever has been, nor ever will be, for you are with us in our rising up, in our going forth, in our coming in, and in our lying down. Through Jesus Christ, our Lord eternal. Amen.

21

We are not prone to think about eternity these days, O God. We are much more absorbed in meeting deadlines—in living by schedules and completing agendas and climbing into bed at night exhausted from the frenetic pace of our daily existence. When we pause as we are doing now and open the windows of our souls to the refreshing breezes from a higher dimension, we realize how we impoverish ourselves by being so committed to our hectic routines and failing to be still at the center of our selves and to listen for the whispers of hope and assurance that there is more and that it is always there for us, if we can only learn to wait and to watch for the signs of your eternal being. Come upon us now, dear God, like a mother tucking her children in bed. Hover over us with a comforting presence and restore us where we are tired and spent and frazzled. Through Jesus our Lord, who instructed us to pray, *Our Father. . . .*

22

Our experiences of you, O God, are always fresh and beautiful. If there is anything missing in this hour, it is because of our own blindness and insensitivity. Forgive us for the days when we have not been aware of your presence, and the hours when we have not paused to thank you for life itself. Let the sparks of hope in the ashes of our past lives now be fanned into open flames again, and our souls warmed by the coming of your divine Spirit. Remind us of important things we have forgotten and reveal the contours of a wonderful future that is both your dream and ours, through Jesus Christ our Savior, who taught us to pray, saying, *Our Father.* . . .

23

If we can trust the love and understanding in one another's faces, O God, how much more can we trust your love and understanding, which have cared for us from before we were born, have watched over us all our days, and surround us now in this place, among all these friends and loved ones, with blessedness and peace. Teach us to relax in that love and understanding and to let it carry us the way the water in an ocean carries a boat. Help us not to try so hard to be smarter than we are or more attractive than we are or more religious than we are, but instead to let your divine energy and love flow through us so freely and abundantly that we cannot help being wise and attractive and spiritual. Enable us in this hour to put away our greatest cares and concerns and to be borne up by your Holy Spirit, which is here to heal and restore us in every way. Through Christ our Lord, who taught us to pray, saying, *Our Father.* . . .

24

An Opening Prayer for Mother's Day or Father's Day

In every age, O God, it has been important to honor the faith of our mothers and fathers. But in some ages, like our own, when the mountains are crashing into the sea and the waters are rising upon the earth, it is also important to go beyond the faith they had, to employ the insights and courage derived from them to read the times we live in and go out to discover new and vital forms for expressing the cherished truths of all the ages. We pray that we may be equal to the task that is ours today, of forging new paths and making new relationships that will even more nearly fulfill the divine will than was ever possible in our parents' lives. Let this be an age of real heroism in the faith, when men and women will risk everything to serve the vision of your kingdom passed on by loved ones in successive generations. And to that end, teach us to pray the prayer that Jesus taught us, saying, *Our Father.* . . .

25

We live in a world where people are always looking for glory and honor, O God, where we seek credit for contributions made, for movies produced, for books published, for favors done. Yet all glory, laud, and honor belong to you alone, for you are the one who has given us this beautiful world and provided our homes and our jobs and our families and our bountiful way of life. Forgive us for ever thinking the credit is ours, or for taking pride in achievements that owe little to us in our own strength and ingenuity. Teach us to live humbly and gratefully, admiring what you have made and being sensitive to what you bestow. Help us to follow simply and honestly in the footsteps of our Master, who taught us to pray, saying, *Our Father.* . . .

26

An Opening Prayer for the Sunday Before Independence Day

There is great beauty in our land, O God, because it is the land you have given us. The knowledge of this makes the hills and plains even more beautiful and enhances our joy in the lakes and rivers, the fields and the mines, and the cities and bridges and highways. All of us together, whether our origins were here or in Europe or Asia or Africa or some other part of the world, are participating members in one of the great families of history, and we know that family owes its greatness to your generous blessing. Grant that in all of the excitement of this holiday, in all the waving of banners and flying of rockets, we shall remember and be greatly thankful. Teach us true humility, in order that our eyes may see all your wonders and we may live our lives with respect to your divine mystery, through Christ Jesus our Lord, who taught us to pray, saying, *Our Father. . . .*

27

Because of you, O God, our lives ought to be a continual rejoicing. Yet we often live in cramped and defeated postures, forgetting the beauty of the world and the richness of love and the glory of merely being alive. Forgive us for every day and hour we have spent in such forgetfulness, and make us sensitive once more to the joy of your eternal presence. Lift the clouds of gloom and sadness from our hearts and help us to thrill at the brightness of this day and our prospects in it. Free us from our preoccupation with ourselves and let us delight in our relationship to the rest of the world, for you have loved the world and sent your Son into the world to redeem and reshape it in his image—your Son, who taught us to pray, saying, *Our Father. . . .*

28

Your newborn creation must have been wonderful, O God, with sunlight breaking through the shreds of mist that still clung to everything! But the creation is still beautiful: hills and plains and valleys, rivers running to the seas, flowers and trees and waving fields of grain, and now cities and highways and bridges, and people everywhere, red, white, black, yellow, and brown, working and playing and rushing from one place to another! You must be very happy with what you have made, except when we fail to love one another or when we adopt a tired and grudging attitude toward the world around us. Teach us to mirror the joy in your own heart, O God, and to be filled with a spirit of love and kindness toward everyone and everything, so that he shall not have lived and died in vain who taught us to pray, saying, *Our Father.* . . .

29

We praise many things in our lifetimes, O God. We praise our parents for loving and caring for us when we were children. We praise our friends for their cleverness and friendship. We praise the companies we work for, for the opportunities and security they give us. We praise schools, political parties, elected officials, restaurants, books, movies, automobiles, even brands of coffee and toothpaste. But there is nothing that deserves praise as you do, O God, for your almighty power, your unquestionable wisdom, and your loving patience with us on our journeys through life. Our small minds cannot begin to comprehend the depth of your being or the breadth of your care. Forgive us that we ponder these things so little and remember them so seldom. Let this be an hour for each of us when our finite spirits are touched by your great eternal Spirit and we begin to live our lives on a new level, with a higher consciousness of your creative presence in our affairs, and we shall learn to praise you with a new voice. Through Christ Jesus our Lord, who taught us to pray, saying, *Our Father.* . . .

30

We live and work and serve in the midst of great beauty, O God—among trees and flowers and gracious homes and gently winding streets and spacious skies. Yet we confess that we often forget to notice the beauty because we are so intent on our struggles to make a living, attend to property, find advancement, raise our children, care for aging parents, and deal with the daily onslaught of human problems. Teach us, we pray, to reserve time each day for centering our lives on you and your creation, and let that time begin slowly but surely to take possession of our minds and hearts, so that we are no longer anxious and care-ridden but can truly enjoy the beauty and glory of the world. Through Christ our Lord, who taught us to pray, saying, *Our Father. . . .*

31

It is hard for us to imagine now, O God, in a world sordid with crime and corruption and terrorism, that you will one day control everything with love and peace and gentleness. But we pray for the grace to believe with all our hearts, and to act out in our own lives the conditions of your kingdom. Make us kind and loving, forgiving of our enemies, and ready to go the second mile. Let us treat others as we would like to be treated. Help us to live with honor and trust and generosity. And show us the importance of even laying down our lives for those who don't believe, in order that your glorious dream of the lion sleeping peacefully with the lamb and the bear eating straw with the ox may truly come on the earth and make brothers and sisters of us all. Through Christ our everlasting Savior, who taught us to pray, saying, *Our Father. . . .*

32

Our hearts are funny things, O God, rising and falling at the oddest moments. We can be encouraged by the smile of a friend but dejected by a few drops of rain. We can become excited by the prospects of a meal but depressed that we ate too much again. Yet there is always something stimulating and enlivening about your presence, and when we become aware of it our hearts seem to glow and be lifted up. We wish we lived more constantly in awareness of your presence, and of the infinite love you want to pour into our lives. Teach us awareness in the midst of distraction, and sensitivity in a world that is often crude and insensitive. Embrace us now with your Spirit, and in the hours to follow let us walk in it so that everything looks different when we leave this place. In the name of Christ our Savior, who taught us to pray, saying, *Our Father. . . .*

33

We live in a world that responds to power, O God: the power of money, the power of celebrity, the power of influence, the power of leverage, the power of weapons. But your power, which the world often fails to understand, is a power beyond any of these, for it is the power of love, a simple power to change hearts and heal wounds and mend broken relationships and gather us all into the eternal community. Forgive us that we have not all learned this, so that we often depend on the other kinds of power instead of yours. Grant that this may be an hour of quiet discovery, in which we feel our hearts being strangely warmed and our spirits drawn irresistibly toward new possibilities and commitments. Whatever our way has been, show us a higher one. Whatever our dreams have been, give us better ones. And we shall continue to praise you, through Christ our Lord, who taught us to pray, saying, *Our Father. . . .*

34

You made the world and the galaxies in unity and harmony, O God, and yet our ancestors never understood how to live in unity and harmony. So you sent your ideal Son among us to restore the original unity and harmony. Yet even he discovered that his coming provoked enmity and warfare and hostility instead of producing oneness. There is a natural perversity in our makeup, O God, that will not let us be what you want us to be. And yet you love us, and continue to tempt us into unity and harmony, into companionship with your heavenly Spirit and togetherness with one another. Forgive us for our waywardness and recalcitrance and draw us more and more into your way, so that the world may see and experience your lovingkindness and the church of our Lord may be redeemed from all its sin. Through Christ Jesus, in whose name we pray, saying, *Our Father. . . .*

THREE

Affirmations of Faith

1

We believe in the love of God that forms the basis for all
   human love:
   the love parents have for their children,
   the love children have for their parents,
   the love of friends who really care,
   and every little act of kindness bestowed as a gift in the
      human community.
We believe that God loved the world through Christ, who
   showed what it means to love another by laying down
   his life for all those who would come after him, even in
   our own time.
We believe that love will eventually triumph in the world,
   despite all envy, hate, and greed, despite wars and
   rumors of war, and despite the fact that it seems so rare.
For love is of God and God is love, and God will not rest
   until all are reconciled in love.

2

I believe in the God of fruit-time and harvest, who makes
   the land to bear gifts in its time and fills our tables with
   bounty;
I believe in Jesus Christ his Son, who was the firstfruit of
   those who slept and brings us to spiritual tables where
   our cups are always full;

I believe in the Holy Spirit, who causes us to remember all
things for which we are grateful and teaches us to see a
relationship between our gifts and the Giver;

I believe in the world as the arena of my spiritual life, where
I am to share my table with the poor and my hospitality
with the stranger; for in so doing I shall fulfill the desires
of the One who has given me everything, and of the Son
and the Holy Spirit as well. Amen.

3

I believe in God Almighty, who sets life before us as a
course to be run and gives us bodies and minds with
which to run it;

I believe in Jesus Christ, his only Son, who has shown us
what it is to run with commitment and has revealed in
his resurrection the reward to those who finish the
course;

I believe in the Holy Spirit, who breathes into us the
strength to run long distances, the wisdom to pace ourselves, and the love to respect all other runners;

I believe in the Church Universal, that gives us a sense of
fellowship as we run, and the feeling that if anything
happens on the course we shall be supported by those
who care;

I believe in the Life Everlasting, where the course we have
run in this life gives way to a course finer than any we
have ever known, and where our spirits shall run with a
grace and beauty we have not yet experienced;

I believe—and because I believe, I run better! Amen.

4

We believe in the God of children, who ordains his truths to
come from the mouths of babes and receives them into
the heavenly kingdom;

We believe in the God of young people, who guides them in the course of their development and calls them into divine service;

We believe in the God of young adults, who blesses them with work for their hands and hope for the world they are building;

We believe in the God of older adults, who forgives their shortcomings, hears their prayers for the young, and helps them to see the beauty of all their relationships;

We believe in the God of the elderly, who prepares them even in this life for the blessedness of the life to come, and whispers in their sleep of the wholeness that awaits them beyond death;

We believe in the God of all ages, who, though being ageless, walks with us in every age; it is God who has made us, and not we ourselves; and God will be with us as the Shepherd of our souls, leading us into green pastures and beside still waters from now to eternity; through Jesus Christ our Lord, to whom be glory forever and ever. Amen.

5

I believe in God, who put music in the universe, so that the birds and the wind, the animals and insects, and the very stars in their courses are the makers of melody.

I believe in Christ, whose message of love and grace enables me to sing from the depths of my being, praising God for my salvation and for the redemption of all who put their trust in him.

I believe in the Holy Spirit, who touches the strings of my life the way a master musician touches the strings of a harp, causing me to produce beautiful resonance in the lives of others.

I believe in worship, not because it is reasonable or sensible but because I can't help it:

My heart sings in response to my faith! Amen.

6

An Affirmation of Faith for the Sunday Before Labor Day

We believe in the God who made heaven and earth, and in
the importance of making as God has made—
of erecting homes and buildings,
of constructing roads and bridges,
of designing planes and cars,
of baking cakes and pies,
of composing music and painting pictures,
of discovering new drugs and medical procedures,
of filling granaries with corn and wheat,
of shaping cities into communities,
of making humanity into what God wants it to be.
We are grateful to the Maker of all for the roles of making
in our own lives, and we affirm that our Savior is known
as the Carpenter, for it is good to worship one who cre-
ates and not one who destroys! Amen.

7

I believe in the God of our fathers and mothers, who speaks
to us out of the past and guides our steps by cherished
traditions.
I believe in the God of now, who is still active in the world
and reveals the divine nature to those who do the divine
will.
I believe in the God of tomorrow, who holds the destiny of
nations in almighty hands and is shaping the future for
the sake of the heavenly kingdom.
For this reason I bow my knee to Christ, who has revealed
the ways of God in our midst, and pledge my allegiance
once more to the church, which keeps alive the ministry
of word and sacrament for the salvation of all people and
the redemption of the poor and needy.
May God help me to do my best each day that I live, to love
those around me, to walk responsibly in the way of

Christ, and to pray for the consummation of the divine will among the nations of the world. Amen.

8

I believe in God, the Father of our Lord Jesus Christ, who created the world and all that is in it;

I believe God regards all people as God's children, whether they confess God's parenthood or not;

I believe God intends the riches of the world, including all food and other necessities of life, to be shared among God's children, the gifted caring for the less gifted and the privileged for the underprivileged;

I believe that in proportion as we acknowledge and fulfill this intention we are conformed to the image of our Lord Jesus Christ, who died to set us free from sin and the love of self;

and I believe that the best time to begin this sharing, whether of food or clothing or gospel, is now, today, when it is fresh on our minds and the needs of God's children are as great as they have ever been in the history of the world. Amen.

9

I dare to believe these things:

that God is the God of all the earth, both the living and the dead;

that God has revealed the divine nature in the man Jesus Christ, in order that we may follow his teachings and come to eternal life;

that the Spirit of Christ is in this place today, inviting us to a greater commitment of our lives and bestowing the power to live in that commitment;

that the Church, for all its shortcomings, is still called to love those who are loved by God and to call to fellowship and forgiveness those who walk in sin and darkness;

that the world of our immediate vision is but a poor shadow

of the world that is to be, where Christ reigns as Lord of Lords and God is All in All. Amen.

10

I believe in the God who made the lakes and the mountains, who shaped the sky and the sea and all who inhabit the earth.

I believe in Jesus Christ, the Divine Servant, whose life and death and resurrection were necessary to remind us of the presence of the Creator in all that is.

I believe in the Holy Spirit of God, who dwells in the hearts of men and women and boys and girls, convicting us of sin and moving us toward love and joy in our lives.

I believe in the church and its ministry to the world, making ways for the Creator, Son, and Holy Spirit to be more real in people's lives.

I believe in the life to come, foreshadowed by the life we are living now, yet far beyond it in every way.

And I believe in the importance of worship for reminding me of all these things and enabling me to recenter my life in the midst of the people of God.

To God be the glory! Amen.

11

I believe in the God who made the earth and all that is in it, the heavens and all that exists in them. The cattle on a thousand hills are God's, and God's are the streams that feed the lakes and seas. There is nothing made that is not God's, for God is the Creator and Ruler of all life.

I believe in Jesus Christ, who was in the beginning and without whom nothing that is was made. Yet he did not esteem himself above the creation, but entered it as a carpenter from Galilee, preaching, teaching, and healing wherever he went. He cares for the world as one who died for it, and for all the persons who inhabit it, regardless of their status, philosophy, or religious affiliation.

I believe in the Holy Spirit of God that still hovers over the face of the earth, nursing all creative impulses and calling us to life in her. She offers us the chance to be partners with God in feeding the hungry, teaching the poor, healing the sick, and bringing salvation to the nations.

I believe in the Church as the fellowship of God's partners, planned by God, bought with the blood of Christ, and nurtured in the life of the Spirit. Its meaning is discovered only as it pursues Christ's mission in the world, and only as I give myself without reservation to its work.

Therefore I devote myself anew to the calling of my faith, to witness to God through the work of the church and the use of everything I have, including my time, my money, my energy, and my influence. It is the least I can do. Amen.

12

An Affirmation of Faith for Christmas

I believe in the meaning of Christmas, and the importance of celebrating it in the church.

I believe in the God at the center of Christmas, whose hope for the world was imagined by seers and foretold by prophets.

I believe in the messengers of God, who speak to human beings in quiet moments and in dreams.

I believe in the pondering spirit of Mary, who knew God was involved in the birth of her child, and in the generosity of Joseph, who could accept the involvement of God with his wife.

I believe in the beauty of the manger, transformed by the coming of Jesus, and in the eligibility of every simple place to be ennobled by his presence.

I believe in shepherds, that they often hear songs of grace and glory not heard by those who lead busier, noisier lives.

I believe in gold, frankincense, and myrrh, and less expensive gifts as well, especially when they are gifts of the heart and not merely tokens of duty or obligation.

But above all I believe in Jesus, without whom there would be no Christmas, and in using this season to discover again my relationship to him, so that for me it will not be just an ordinary Christmas, but a time of great joy that will change my life. I too would be born in the stable. Amen.

13
An Affirmation of Faith for Palm Sunday

I believe in the Christ who rode in triumph, but I also believe in the Christ who died on Calvary. I believe in the God who speaks in fire and storm, but I also believe in the God of the still, small voice. I believe that being a Christian involves more than coming to church and being "nice"; I believe it means being faithful in school or business, and worshiping Christ in my private moments. I believe that the real triumphs of Christ are often small and unnoticed, occurring in the lives and decisions of people whose names will never appear in the newspapers. I believe that the best thing I can do for him today is not to say "I believe," but to act out my belief in love and justice for others. For his is no hypocritical kingdom, but a kingdom of truth and reality that shall be forever and ever. Amen.

14
An Affirmation of Faith for Easter Day

We believe in the wildness of Easter, when strong winds blow through the earth and the swollen tips of plants are bursting forth with life, when the logic of all life is challenged by talk of resurrection and return.

We believe in the power of God to contradict our naive assumptions and overturn our natural expectations by raising Christ from the dead again even in the apathy of our modern lives.

We believe in the presence of the risen Christ, who is here now in the community of faith, smiling in the faces of children, nurturing the hopes of the elderly, and challenging us to deny the finality of death.

He did not die in vain.

God made him the firstfruits of those who slept.

God made the rejected stone the foundation of everything.

God swept a mighty hand across our Scrabble boards
    and planted a wildness in our hearts that will not go away.

It is the wildness of Easter, and it means that nothing will ever again be the same, that death itself has died, and that those who are in Christ will live forever.

Hallelujah! We praise God for the wildness that won't go away!

15

I believe in the God of autumn, who spreads the mantle of divine glory across the hills like a cloak of many colors;

I believe in the God of winter, who whispers in the wind and makes me thankful for the warmth of my hearth and blanket;

I believe in the God of spring, who dazzles the eye with blankets of blossoms and speaks to my heart through gentle rains;

I believe in the God of summer, who meets me in the morning mists and waits for me in the cool of the evening;

I believe in the God of all seasons, who is a God for all seasons, and who calls me forth to be a man or woman for all seasons, ready to sacrifice for truth and to love the world as God loves it. God has revealed the divine nature in Jesus Christ and continues to reveal that nature in the world, in history, and in the inner life.

God's name is to be praised forever and ever. Amen.

16

An Affirmation of Faith Based on the Lord's Prayer

I believe in the kingdom of God and in doing God's will here on earth as nearly as possible in the way the angels in heaven must do it, preferring everyone else's good before their own and praising God constantly for the wisdom and beauty of God's indescribable Self.

I believe in asking God each day for the bread my body requires that day, and nothing else; for everything beyond the simplest food and drink is an extravagance of which I am not worthy, especially in a world where so many are hungry and so much of what I used to want now seems to me excessive.

I believe also in remembering my unworthiness before God and asking for forgiveness, not only for unkind words I've thought or spoken and for behaving ungenerously toward others but also for all the things I should have thought or done or spoken, the little loving and encouraging signs that would have made the world a better place.

And I believe in praying to avoid the trial or temptation of my faith beyond my power to recognize and resist the Tempter, whose disguises are legion and whose facility for infiltrating my defenses is beyond the limited power of my imagination.

God is God, and I, well, I am only me, and I am grateful that the One whose power and glory and kingdom can never, ever fail has acted graciously in my behalf to save me from my own shortcomings and give me a place in the eternal Community, together with the saints of all the ages.

It is a gift beyond belief—which is why I must daily say "I believe" and try to remember that it is so. Amen.

FOUR

Prayers of Confession

1

O God, who brooded over the world when it was created and broods now over your children until we are shaped in the image of Christ, we confess our daily sins: the word sharply spoken, the praise withheld, the embrace not given, the hurt disguised, the envy felt, the self indulged, the need neglected. Receive us now broken, penitent, wishing it were otherwise. Enfold us in the arms of love and forgiveness and restore a new spirit within us. Make us one with ourselves, with each other, with the world, with time and all the saints. Let your name be magnified, let Christ be glorified, let the Holy Spirit be intensified, in each heart and on all our lips, this day and forever. Amen.

2

I admit to you, O God, that I am often distressed by the daily news: by the failure of nations to agree, by the insistent problems of hunger and war and economy, by crime and negligence and immorality. I wish my sense of the presence of Christ were strong and I had more confidence in his eternal victory over the world. Then I would not be shaken by the winds of adversity but would stand like a tree planted by the living waters. Forgive my weakness and deepen my faith, through Jesus Christ our Lord. Amen.

Leader: This is a true word and worthy of all acceptance:
People: **He has borne our shortcomings, and by his stripes we are healed;**

Leader: He has carried captivity captive and won our devotion forever.

People: **The Lord's name be praised forever and ever! Amen.**

3

We confess to you, O God, that we have used only a small part of the potential that is in us: There are energies, powers, and possibilities in us that have never been released. Forgive us for settling for second best, for growing accustomed to the way we think and act, and then failing to go beyond our usual responses. Help us to yield to you this day, and thus to open our lives once more to joy, service, and adventure. Amen.

Leader: God is the creator of all that is.

People: **God wants to create the future with us.**

Leader: It is up to us to surrender to God's leadership and contribute to the future.

People: **This is the real meaning of forgiveness, to know we have surrendered to God. Amen.**

4

We confess to you, O God, that we are not the persons we would like others to think we are. We are not even the persons we would like to think of ourselves as being. Only in the security of your love are we able to admit our secret fears and desires. Hear them now, O God, and forgive us for our duplicity. Give us new life from above and reshape us in the image of Christ, who is the One we would really like to resemble. For his name's sake. Amen.

Leader: Christ has died for our sins and failures.

People: **His death atones for all our inadequacies.**

Leader: God receives us now in love and forgiveness.

People: **In love and forgiveness, God helps us to become what we ought to be. Amen.**

5

We acknowledge, O God, that we have strayed like lost sheep from the path and have not sought your will in our lives. We have cared more for pleasure than for righteousness and have sought our own welfare instead of the welfare of others. We are empty and unhappy without you. Receive us in penitence and forgive our sins, through Jesus Christ our Lord. Amen.

Leader: Christ was wounded for our transgressions;
People: **He was bruised for our iniquities.**
Leader: The Lord has laid on him the chastisement of our peace,
People: **And by his stripes we are healed.**
Leader: I assure you that God, for Christ's sake, has forgiven our sin. Amen.

6

We admit, O God, the idolatries of our hearts. We fasten upon things temporal instead of things eternal. We follow our own desires instead of seeking your will. In a world of pain and suffering, we do little to alleviate them. Forgive us, O God, and put a right spirit within us. Help us love the unlovely and care for the brokenhearted. Use us to bless the world around us. Through Jesus Christ our Lord. Amen.

Leader: God has revealed the divine nature to us in Jesus Christ.
People: **God will forgive our sin if we honestly try to follow the way of Christ.**
Leader: If we confess our sin, God will lift us up and restore us to the way of righteousness.
People: **God will help us to live in the Spirit and not in the flesh. Amen.**

7

We are not worthy, O God, to call on your name. We have failed in our attempts to carry out your law. We have not loved you above everything in our lives, and we have not loved one another more than ourselves. It is only by the goodness of your will that we live from day to day and are gathered here today to worship in the name of Christ. Pardon our iniquities and cleanse us of secret faults, that we may go forth to glorify your presence in the earth. Through him who loved you and taught us to call you our Father. Amen.

Leader: God's mercy is from everlasting to everlasting.
People: **God receives us as a father receives his wayward children.**
Leader: God deals with us as a mother deals with those she loves.
People: **In God's love we are set free from the past and can act upon the future in new ways.**
Leader: We are free to care about the things that matter.
People: **We are free to live! Amen.**

8

O God, you are like a parent who cares for the welfare of the family. We often behave like thoughtless, selfish children. We want the best of everything for ourselves, without considering our brothers and sisters. We are reluctant to invest our time and energy for the benefit of others. Forgive us, O God, and let the family become more important to us. Help us be like Christ, who gave up everything for the sake of the kingdom. Amen.

Leader: If God is our parent, then God loves us in spite of ourselves.
People: **God desires our wholeness, not our punishment.**
Leader: Therefore let us look for the good things God wishes to give us.
People: **God bless us with love and acceptance. Amen.**

9

I seek your forgiveness, O God, for the hold of cynicism on my life; for the way I distrust the motives of others, attributing to them the darkness of my own thoughts; for the skepticism with which I hear the biblical word and the stories of others' faith; for my failure to believe that you can make my life new and beautiful this day and cause me to live with power and joy. Sometimes my life is a misery, dear God, because of my unbelief. Help me to be committed to you and to find delight and innocence through purity of heart. For your love's sake. Amen.

Leader: Our God is just, like the way of an honest judge.
People: **But God is also tender, like the heart of a mother beholding her child.**
Leader: God will forgive our sin and pardon our iniquity.
People: **God will bind up our wounds and pour oil on our troubled spirits.**
Leader: In the name of Christ, we are forgiven for all our wrongs.
People: **Let us rise up in newness of life, and praise God's name! Amen.**

10

Ever-loving God, who knows the secrets of our hearts even when they are a puzzle to us, we admit to you the problems in our natures. We are seldom satisfied with what we have in life. We long for what others have, though we would soon become bored with it if it were ours. We do not realize our real worth and would like to be admired and famous. We often miss the simple gifts of every day because we are searching for what we do not have. Teach us to wait before you in prayer. Open our eyes and ears to the beauty and mystery of what is ours. Give us wholeness in your kingdom, through Jesus Christ our Lord. Amen.

Leader:	We have the word of the scriptures that God loves us and wants only the best for us.
People:	**God wants us to be whole and loving and at peace with ourselves.**
Leader:	God has given us his only Son to die on the cross.
People:	**Surely God has forgiven our sins and will heal our brokenness. Amen.**

11

Because we have always had enough to eat, O God, we have taken food for granted. We cannot really put ourselves in the place of those who have less than a handful of grain each day or lie awake at night with gnawing in their stomachs. Forgive us for the breads and cakes we enjoy while others hunger, and the meats and casseroles we devour while they die of starvation. Let us have mercy upon them as you have had mercy upon us. Let us find ways of sharing the bounty of your hand. Through Jesus Christ, who said, "Just as you did it to one of the least of these who are members of my family, you did it to me."* Amen.

Leader:	God has always shown mercy on those who themselves show mercy.
People:	**God will hear us if we earnestly repent and seek a better way.**
Leader:	For what does the Lord require of us, but to do justice, to love mercy,
All:	**And to walk humbly with our God. Amen.**

12

A Confession of Sin for the Opening of the School Year

As the world turns to another year of education, O God, we admit that we have studied too little about you. We have

* Matthew 25:40.

learned math and languages but have not counted the cost of serving Christ or learned to listen to your still, small voice. We have memorized facts from history books but have not dwelled enough on the history of your faithfulness. We have learned much about chemistry but have been too little interested in the chemistry of our relationship with you. Forgive us, O God, for trusting in our own knowledge, and help us to rely more upon the knowledge of you that we have received in our Lord Jesus Christ. Amen.

Leader: God knows the hearts of men and women.
People: **If we pray in sincerity, God will hear our prayers.**
Leader: God will hear from heaven and will forgive our sin.
People: **Let us rejoice in the power of forgiven sins!**
Leader: We are all, for Christ's sake, forgiven.

13

Compared with your will, O God, our ways are crooked and not straight; our desires are selfish and not generous; our devotion is shallow and not deep. We have used your name without seriousness and have lived without gratitude for all your gifts. Forgive us, we ask, and turn our hearts to true repentance. Let the spirit of Christ convert and dwell in us, that we may honor you with our entire beings. For your name's sake. Amen.

Leader: God is a God of holiness and justice.
People: **God is also a God of mercy and forgiveness.**
Leader: God has promised to forgive our sin if we devoutly ask it.
People: **God will hear our prayer and take away our guilt, in the name of Christ our Lord. Amen.**

14

We confess, O God, that we have been less than childlike in our minds and hearts. We have labored for that which does not satisfy, and given ourselves to things that do not build up the family of God. Our hearts have been anxious for rank and personal welfare, and not for the coming of your kingdom. Forgive us, we pray, and redeem us from all our sin. In the name of the everlasting Savior, Jesus Christ our Lord. Amen.

Leader:	Christ has borne our sins and carried our sorrows.
People:	**He has loved us when we were unworthy of love.**
Leader:	Surely God has forgiven us for Christ's sake, and made us children of the promise.
People:	**God has heard our prayer and will receive us in love and rejoicing. Amen.**

15

My life becomes enmeshed in the things of this world, O God: I worry about money and property and having enough. I am anxious about taxes, high prices, and inflation rates. My standard of living is more affected by Madison Avenue than by the Bible, and my model of behavior is more likely to come from Hollywood than from Jesus. Forgive me, O God, and restore me to a sense of my higher commitments. Let your presence mean more to me than a new car or a handful of money-market certificates or a lifetime annuity; for you are my life, my strength, and my salvation. Amen.

Leader:	God's heart is like the cedars rising above the wilderness.
People:	**God's forgiveness is plentiful, and God's mercy is abundant.**
Leader:	God hears us when we pray and forgives us when we earnestly repent.
People:	**Surely goodness and mercy will follow us all the days of our lives, and we shall dwell in the house of the LORD forever. Amen.***

---

* Psalm 23, author's paraphrase.

16

When we consider the cross, O God, we realize what poor stewards we have been. We have divided what you gave us into "ours" and "theirs," and cared for others only when it suited us. We have turned your gifts into personal possessions, instead of seeing them as gifts for all. Forgive us, O God, and restore us to a Christlike philosophy of life. Amen.

Leader: God has given the divine Spirit as a witness in our midst.

People: **God corrects us when we take the wrong path or adopt a poor attitude.**

Leader: This is because God wants us to experience what is best for us.

People: **God loves us and restores us to fellowship in the divine community. Amen.**

17

We call you light, O Lord, yet walk in darkness. We call you love, yet despise those who are unlike ourselves. We call you joy, yet live in depression and unhappiness. Forgive us, dear Lord, and convert us to your way. Let the power of your salvation change us into the people we were meant to be, that your light and love may fill our lives forever and we may praise your name with our whole hearts. Through Jesus Christ. Amen.

Leader: God loves us even at the worst times of our lives.

People: **God never leaves us to make it on our own.**

Leader: God has promised to forgive us and help us whenever we truly repent and seek his heavenly will.

People: **God will restore us to the joy of our salvation and strengthen us for living in divine grace. Amen.**

18
A Prayer of Confession for Advent

I am not ready, O God, for the coming of Christ into my life. There is much I am not prepared to surrender. I do not want to give up home or family or friends to follow him. I cherish my possessions, and do not choose to share them with others. I like being my own master, even though I do not manage it very well, and am reluctant to submit completely to your will. It would be a great favor to me if you would lead me out of my selfishness and into your love. For yours really is the kingdom and the power and the glory forever. Amen.

Leader:	The coming of Christmas is a reminder of God's desire for all humanity.
People:	**It recalls God's involvement in human history.**
Leader:	It says that God really cares about us and forgives our sins.
People:	**It means that God will answer our prayers and save us from ourselves. Amen.**

19
A Prayer of Confession for Palm Sunday

O Lord, we have sinned against you in word, in thought, and in action. We have not walked in the ways you have taught us, or worshiped you in the wholeness of our hearts. We have sung praises to you when the crowds were singing, but have not followed you in the suffering of Calvary. Forgive us for our unfaithfulness, and give us the spirit of true repentance. For yours is the kingdom of love and mercy. Amen.

Leader:	God's heart is always open when we confess our sin.

People: **God will receive our prayers and bless the intentions of our hearts.**

Leader: God's mercy is from everlasting to everlasting.

People: **God's lovingkindness is to all generations— including ours! Amen.**

20

A Prayer of Confession for Maundy Thursday

Why do I always feel guilty, Lord, when I hear about Judas? Is it because I too am like him, taking every opportunity to betray you? I am sorry, Lord; I live in a world where betrayal is the norm; where people think of themselves first; where friendship always has a limit; where love is something given on condition; where circumstances always provide a loophole. I wish it were otherwise, and that all people were faithful; that trust were the expected and not the unexpected thing; that my love could be counted on, whatever happens. What a different world it would be— like the kingdom of love you described. Renew my vision, Lord, of your faithfulness to us. Help me to recommit myself to the way of the cross. For even with its pain and suffering, your way is better than my way, and your love is stronger than my betrayal. Amen.

Leader: There is a wideness in God's mercy, like the wideness of the sky.

People: **There is a depth in God's mercy, like the depth of the sea.**

Leader: Surely God will receive us when we turn from our sin.

People: **God will hear us and forgive us, even as the thief was forgiven on the cross.**

Leader: May God have mercy on us.

People: **May God indeed have mercy on us! Amen.**

21

With the coming of spring, O God, we are aware of ourselves as gardens. We have lain fallow through the winter, our souls untended. Reminders of an old life still clutter the surfaces of our lives. Things dormant in us are beginning to grow. We stretch toward the sunlight, with gratitude for the warmth. We wait to be tilled, to have the hard earth broken and made soft again. We long for the gentle rains of your Spirit to give life to the good things inside us. We lament the weeds that grow in spite of all our best wishes. Come, O God, and renew the life that is in us. Raise us up to fruitfulness in your kingdom. We pray in the name of Jesus Christ, who came as the Son of the Most High Gardener. Amen.

Leader: God is a tender care that nothing be lost.
People: **Not even the tenderest young shoot in the garden.**
Leader: God gives life where there was death, and hope where there was despair.
People: **Surely God will forgive our sins and have mercy upon us.**
Leader: God will strengthen us in our inward being.
People: **God will deliver us into the kingdom of the Divine Servant! Amen.**

22

In a world where we are surrounded by knowledge, O God, we confess that we have known too little about you. We have been so busy learning about geography and mathematics and sociology that we have neglected our souls. We have expanded our horizons with courses and journals and special seminars but have not deepened our understanding of life itself. We have mastered computer programs and management styles and getting around on freeways but have not learned how to pray and live daily in your presence. Forgive us, dear God, and help us to become knowledgeable about the things that truly matter. Amen.

Leader: Life is best when it is lived with God.

People: **God will forgive us for the mistakes we've made.**

Leader: Mistakes are bad only if we don't learn from them.

People: **We can rejoice in our forgiveness, for it helps us to know God better. Amen.**

23

You have given us so much, O God, and we have given you so little. You have given us hearts for love, and we have thought mostly of ourselves. You have given us bodies for work and play and service, and we have abused them with food and neglect. You have given us homes and money and everything we need, and we have shared little with others. You have given us spirits for contemplation, and we have seldom engaged in prayer. Have mercy upon us, O God, and set us on the right path again. Give us your Spirit and help us to give our whole selves to you. Amen.

Leader: When we have sinned, God wants only our restoration.

People: **Surely God hears us when we pray for forgiveness.**

Leader: Now we must commit to living out what we have asked.

People: **Otherwise our prayers are hollow, and our hearts will be empty. Amen.**

FIVE

Offertory Prayers

1

When we love, O God, we want to give. We would give away our very lives if we loved enough. It is out of our love for you and the world you have made that we turn now to the act of worship through giving. Let these love offerings of our hearts reach out into all the world, saving lives and making life more worthwhile, through Jesus Christ our Lord. Amen.

2

We hope, O God, that you enjoy gifts as much as we do. We thank you for all the gifts you have given us and bring these gifts now as a sign of our love and good will toward you. Grant, as with all our gifts, that they may be used wisely and well, and that your name may be glorified, through Jesus Christ. Amen.

3

In this setting, O God, our hearts become full of your spirit, and we are reminded of the many gifts that constitute our daily lives. Now we offer to you this small bit of who we are and what we have as a way of saying, "Thank you, we love you, God." Amen.

4

Whatever we give to you, O God, is but a small reflection of the bounty you have bestowed on us. Teach us generosity with all we have, including our love and praise, that we may live abundantly as Christ did. Amen.

5

Even a committee of our most sensitive members, O God, could not begin to enumerate the countless treasures with which you have endowed our existence: beauties of nature, miracles of health and well-being, gifts of love and family and friends. At the very least, each of us owes you a spirit of gratitude, and we pray for your Holy Spirit to enrich our hearts and minds in ways to remind us of that, now and in all our days to come. Through Jesus Christ. Amen.

6

Our lives are filled with your blessings, O God: the air we breathe, the food we eat, the homes we live in, the health that permits us to be here, the people we love who also love us. Grant that we may never live insensitively but may praise and worship you endlessly for your goodness. Now let your blessing be upon the small gifts we have made, that they may be used wisely and graciously for your kingdom's sake. Amen.

7

In and of ourselves, O God, we are fragmented, and our gifts are only partial. But in you we become whole, and our giving is whole. Receive now the love and worship and money that reflect who we have come to be—or who we have yet to become—in your kingdom. Through Jesus Christ our Lord. Amen.

8

You have given us this day, O God, and the minds and hearts to enjoy it. We cannot help thinking of those whose bodies are wracked by suffering, whose minds are twisted by grief, whose beings are imprisoned by class or poverty or other tyrannies. Teach us sensitivity and gratitude, and let us thank you now in the generosity of our offerings. Amen.

9

The hand takes, O God, and the hand gives away. Help us to give as freely as we have learned to take, and to worship you in doing it. Through Jesus Christ. Amen.

10

There is your business, O God, and there is the world's business. Help us to know the difference and to do your business here, that in so doing we may make the world's business your business. Through Jesus Christ. Amen.

11

We have so much for which to be thankful, O God: our homes, our loved ones, our work, our friends, our strength, our daily bread. Help us not to be thoughtless and take these things for granted, but most of all, help us not to take for granted your great salvation, given to us in Jesus Christ. Let the gifts we bring now be mere symbols of our gratitude and love. In our Master's name. Amen.

12
An Offertory Prayer for Thanksgiving

In this season of thanksgiving, O God, we remember all your gifts to us, especially the gift of your Son, who died to save us from our sin. May his name be exalted through this offering as it finds its way to many parts of the world, slaking thirst, assuaging hunger, healing sickness, and filling the souls of those who wait to hear your Word. Amen.

13

You have always outgiven us, O Lord, and you have done it again today. But accept these gestures of our love for you and our concern for others, that we may be blessed in the very act of giving. For Christ's sake. Amen.

14

Our gifts are small and inadequate, O God, in comparison with the gift of life in Christ Jesus. But we offer them now in loving faith and obedience, desiring to please you and serve you forever, our Maker and Redeemer and Friend. Amen.

15

It is godlike, O Lord, to be a giver, for you have shown us the model for all giving by sending your Son to die for the sins of the world. Teach us each day to be more generous, that we may not feel strangely awkward in your presence when we die. Through Christ our Lord. Amen.

16

We praise you, Father, Son, and Holy Spirit, for the richness of our lives and the gift of this time of worship. Accept now these partial offerings of our hearts, and let all else follow, until we are fully yours, in Christ Jesus our Lord. Amen.

17

We thank you, O God, that you have put a spirit of giving into our hearts. Grant that the gifts we have now brought to you will be only the first of many gifts we shall give to others in the course of this week, out of love for them and remembrance of your many mercies to us. Through Jesus our Lord. Amen.

18

Whenever we wonder what we should give to you, O God, remind us of what you have given us in Christ Jesus and what he gave for the grace and freedom we now enjoy; and help us to include among the recipients of our own gifts, as he did, those in the poorest position to repay us. For your name's sake. Amen.

19

We have enjoyed many gifts since the last time we were here, O God. Help us to remember them now and to make this offering to you in joy and gratitude. For you are the giver of every good and perfect gift, and we are but children learning to imitate your generosity. Amen.

20

We love you, O God, and we love your world. Therefore we bring our gifts, and pray that they may be lovingly used to bring light in the darkness and comfort to your little ones, here and throughout the world. In Christ's name. Amen.

21

Our lives are filled with the sunshine of your love and presence, O God, with love and joy and gifts beyond naming. We choose now to share the sunshine with others, giving from our hearts and substance to assist others in our human community, and to make your name known in all the earth. Through Jesus Christ our Lord. Amen.

22

There is nothing in our hands, O God, that was not given by you. Yet we bring our gifts like faithful servants and hold them up for your blessing. Through Christ our Lord. Amen.

23

You have overflowed our lives, O God, with gifts of love and kindness. Everything of worth we have ever had has come from you. Now teach us to live with grateful hearts, that we may value the Giver more than the gifts, and be faithful to you with joyous spirits. Through Jesus our Lord. Amen.

24

We are surely the most bountifully gifted people in the world, O God, with too much to eat and too many rooms in our houses and too many things in our closets. Make us ever mindful of those in the world who have so little, and in the shock of gratitude, let us begin to care for them with what you have entrusted to us. Through Christ our Lord. Amen.

25

There is always something special, O God, about the moment when we bring our offerings to the altar, for every gift represents a heart that has been touched in some way by your goodness. Receive our gifts, therefore, in the gladness and humility with which they are given and know that we really love you. Amen.

26

If we have thankful spirits, O Lord, we can spend our entire day in praise and thanksgiving for all the gifts with which you have surrounded us: the world of nature, the joy of family and friends, the warmth of fellowship, the beauty of art, the taste of food, the merriment of the heart. Our gifts in this offering are but small tokens of our gratitude for everything you are and do for us, and we bring them now with the prayer that they may be used for the celebration of your kingdom as it breaks in upon our lives, and indeed upon all the world. Through Jesus Christ our Lord. Amen.

27

Most of us have given you very little, O God, for we are not accustomed to living with the generosity you have shown to us. But we offer these gifts to you with praise and thanksgiving, and with the prayer that this week will be filled with opportunities to share with those around us the multiple blessings of our lives in Christ. For his name's sake. Amen.

28

No gift is really a gift, O God, until the heart says it is a gift. Help each one of us to lift up our hearts now and bless your name for all you have done for us individually and as a community. Through Christ our Lord. Amen.

29

In a place as beautiful as this, O Lord, and on a day as fair, what can we give you that will gladden your heart as you have gladdened ours? Only our loving obedience, which we hope is embodied in these humble offerings. Through Christ our Lord. Amen.

30

Like little children, O God, we bring our gifts to our heavenly Parent, and feel a tremor of excitement that we are able to give you something made with our own hands and ingenuity. Look with favor upon our gifts, we pray, and send us forth with the desire to continue this act by giving to others, through Christ our Lord. Amen.

31

How awful it would be, dear God, if we never felt gratitude for the wonderful blessings of our lives—for homes and food and work and loved ones and faith and fellowship. Please accept these gifts as small reminders of our thanksgiving and make us ever more sensible of our bounty through Christ our Lord. Amen.

32

You have given us an unbelievable world, O God, of lakes and rivers and flowers and trees and laughing birds and wide-eyed children. Now we bring our gifts and ask for hearts of sensitivity and gratitude in order that we may properly celebrate it and revel in your love. Through Jesus Christ. Amen.

33

Every week we do this, O God, and it is so easy to look upon it as a meaningless ritual. Yet it is the time when we respond to your measureless love and generosity to us by bringing our offerings to you, and it should fill us with great joy and excitement, for we owe everything to you. Make us sensitive and wise to the most important things in life, we pray, through Jesus Christ our Lord. Amen.

34

It is said that money will not buy happiness, dear God, and that is very true. But our money is a symbol for our work and our striving and our creativity in life, and as such it often represents our deepest feelings. Therefore we dedicate this offering to you and hope you will receive it as a token of our great respect for you and your place in our lives. Through Jesus Christ our Lord. Amen.

35

We cannot begin to enumerate all your blessings, O Lord, since we were last together. When we assemble an offering like this, it is but a small way of saying "Thank you" for everything you've done for us and given us, and of praising you for your great love and power, through Jesus Christ our Lord. Amen.

36

We thank you for the spirit of generosity that flows from you, O God, for you are the one who has taught us to value everything by love and compassion and never by material standards alone. Receive these gifts in that same spirit and enable us to live even more generously this week than we did the week before. Through Jesus Christ. Amen.

37

We are surely gifted above any people in the history of the world, O God, for you have surrounded us with beauty and comfort and love, and have given us everything we need in order to live with grace and happiness. Only crown your gifts with thankfulness, we pray, that we may always live sensitively and humbly and in a reasonable awareness of our great debt to you, our Maker, Redeemer, and Friend. Amen.

38

How unspeakably you have blessed us, O God, with all material things and with the loving fellowship of all these friends. Now bless us with a spirit of gratitude, and help us to spend this week as a continued offering to your grace. Through Christ our Lord. Amen.

SIX

Pastoral Prayers

1

O God, by whose grace we have come to this hour, we thank you for life itself, for sensitivity to light and sound and pressure, for thoughts and memories and anticipation, for love and joy and even for sadness. Forgive us for greed and lust and envy and hate and all other distortions of healthy attitudes. Help us in this hour to be so aware of your presence that it will begin a healing process in us and lead to our total conversions, whereby we think only in purity, act only in kindness, and live only in contentment and gratitude. We offer prayers for our friends who have been touched by death or illness or misfortune. Let their trust in you be perfected by the ministry of the Holy Spirit in their hearts. Continue to bless the efforts of those who would bring peace to our troubled world and fullness of life to all its citizens. Give new courage and vision to the artists and poets of our time, that they may light the way to new understanding in all the nations. Teach us to hear and understand your word for each of us and to become your witnesses through the sharing of this joy for which Christ has died and been raised up forever and ever. Amen.

2

O God, whose life is our peace and whose love is our hope, we wait before you in quietness and humility. Let your mantle fall upon us like a gossamer veil, touching us in all our needs. Lift the burdens of the tired. Still the hearts of the fearful. Encourage the desperate. Ennoble the weak. Give vision to those whose lives are dull, and joy to those who dwell in sadness. Let the sick receive healing and the eager find wisdom. Let the Spirit of Christ abide with us to reveal the true nature of things: the fickleness of popularity, the worthlessness of riches, the value of authenticity, and the pricelessness of love. Grant us the power to live in the world without loving it more than we love you, and to live in you without loving you more than we do your little ones. Make us willing servants of the poor, the very young, and the very old, and let us walk among them as Christ did, bringing hope and dignity to their lives. Teach us to see the abundance of what you have given us and the little we need for daily living; and let the surplus become yours for sharing with the world. Through him who loved us and gave himself for us in pain and sacrifice, Jesus our Lord. Amen.

3

O God, whose name is above every name and whose love goes beyond all that we have ever hoped or believed or expected, we bow our heads in your presence and confess our need of you. Apart from you, our ways become crooked and our instincts unreliable. Let your Spirit fall fresh upon us, that we may walk with you in newness of heart and mind. Recreate our relationships with one another, that we may live in love and thoughtfulness. Show us how to be just in our actions, that none may be hurt by them. Teach us to live each day in humility and simple faith, finding joy in all your gifts. Hear our prayers for the sick or disabled in our community, that they may receive strength and courage, and for the poor, that we may be led in our plenty to care for them. Grant peace and goodwill to the leaders of our nation, that they may conduct our world into new patterns of caring and work for the prosperity of all peoples. Inspire all who hold corporate responsibility in our city and elsewhere to wield their influence for the sake of the common good and not for personal gain or power. Touch those who control the media that they may strive for the uplifting of all humanity and not for mere profit or sensationalism. Anoint the hearts of all teachers, that they may teach their students to search diligently for truth and godliness throughout their lives. Safeguard your church, that it may live above pettiness and contentiousness, and that all your little ones may be led to a fuller experience of your grace and presence. Now expel from our midst all evil thoughts and ways, and gather us together in the warmth and joy of the gospel of Christ, that we may fulfill your desires for us and sing your praises forever and ever, with all the saints and angels, both past, present, and yet to come. Amen.

4

O Lord, you know the unseen burdens with which some of us struggle this morning. There are children here afraid of school, feeling that they are disliked by their teachers and fellow students. There are young people wondering about drugs and drinking and sex, and what is right for them to do in the difficult world of their teens. There are women worried about their appearance in a society that puts a premium on looking right, and men who fear that they don't measure up to the expectations laid on them by family members and employers. There are some who worry about becoming successes in life and others who have become successes and now worry about the meaning of existence. Help all of us, O Lord, whatever the nature of our burdens or struggles, to hear you say, "Come unto me, all you who labor and are heavy laden, and I will give you rest. Take my yoke upon you and learn of me, for I am meek and lowly of heart."* You have indeed been meek and lowly of heart, O Christ, coming among us in a life like our own. Enable us and all our friends and loved ones to come to you and to find, when we are with you, that our perspectives on our

---

* Matthew 11:28-29 KJV, author's paraphrase.

burdens change. Everything changes, O Lord, when we are in you. Therefore draw us and our world to you, and let the new age of your kingdom begin in us, for yours are indeed the kingdom and the power and the glory forever. Amen.

5

O God, we often feel that the road we are traveling is the loneliest road in the world. We cannot imagine that others hurt as much as we hurt. We cannot believe that they long as much as we do for understanding and compassion, or that they feel as handicapped to make a modest success of their lives. Our isolation, our confusion, our depression, our grief seems greater than anyone has ever known. And then we remember our Savior and the lonely road he walked. He was tempted in every way as we are tempted. In the end, everybody deserted him and he was put to death as a common criminal, mocked and tortured and abused. And you raised him up, O God; you glorified him in spite of the lonely road he walked. Help us to identify with him; to hear him calling to us in the crowd; to follow him in the way of the cross. Turn us from our lonely way into his lonely way. Let the power and the glory that were in him be in us. Give us eyes to see what you are doing in the world and to be your servants where you need us. Use us to touch the lives of other persons walking lonely roads. Take what we have to combat hunger and injustice and evil in the earth. Like the heroes of our faith in every age, let us become faithful followers in Christ's way. Make us courageous, generous, loving, and caring, so that one day there may be no lonely road for anyone, but that all may be gathered together in adoration around your throne, sanctified forever and ever by the blood of the One who walked this way before, even Jesus the crucified. Amen.

6

O Holy One, who knows what we desire before we ask and gives it before we think it, we incline our hearts to you in love and gratitude. There are no words to express your goodness, no pictures to describe your infinite care. Teach us how to relax in your presence—how to breathe deeply and know that you are here among us. Let the sense of your coming smooth our wrinkled brows, release the tightness from our muscles, and recondition our thinking about ourselves and the world around us. Shape us to your generosity, that we may love one another with Christlike love, and that we may plan together how best to serve little children in dark, unhappy lands, and lonely, unwed mothers in our own cities, and frightened elder citizens who can no longer cope with a changing world. Grant that the vision of your kingdom may overcome every selfish vision and fear we have, so that we shall be willing to follow our Master even to a cross for the sake of the life to come for all people. Shake us, torment us, and comfort us until we are yours, until we stop playing church and say, "Here I am, Lord; I am yours to command." Then we shall bless your name with all the saints and angels in heaven, and sing your praises forever. Amen.

7

O God, we thank you for the love that cradles us all the days of our lives; for the quietness of our times alone, and the enthusiasm of our times together; for the things we see with our eyes and the things we see with our minds; for the seasons of life, each with its challenge and each with its gifts; for the witness of the poets and artists, who show us the beauty and the music of the world; and for the witness of the saints, who see not only the world but the Spirit beyond it, touching it, shaping it, preparing it for eternity. Let us love the world in the highest sense, so that we care for its beauties and treasures and pass them on to future generations; and let us love your Spirit, so that our inner beings are daily moved toward their real center in your heavenly kingdom. Teach us to submit to your will, both in discipline and supplication, so that, even in illness, we may find wholeness in you. And grant that in every way we may prefer one another's welfare to our own, even as Christ preferred ours to his when he accepted death on the cross. Let the joy of your presence break upon us like a gentle, cloudless sunrise with birds singing, that our spirits may soar to you in simple wonder. For yours is the gift of eternal life. Amen.

8

O God of infinite and tender mercies, we gather before you today in the shadow and gloominess of the rain to confess that there is also shadow and gloominess in our spirits. We are so limited, dear God, that even a change in the weather affects our souls. Therefore we give thanks for your unchangingness, for the light that never dims and the warmth that never cools. Teach us to find in you a refuge from the alterations that cast our spirits up or down, a place of safety and security where our hearts are always touched by joy and hope. Some of us are not well this morning; our bodies are suffering from disease or brokenness beyond our power of healing. Anoint us, O God, with your spirit, that our minds and hearts may transcend our afflictions, emitting some mysterious energy that will meet our needs of both soul and body. Others of us suffer from fear, depression, a sense of confusion or rejection. Anoint us as well, and minister to our downcast spirits. Lift us this hour on wings of faith, that, seeing your kingdom and its promises for our life, we may find new heart and excitement in everyday events. Be gracious to the leaders of the world, and grant them peace in their own hearts, that they may lead their peoples to peace and cooperation. Let the love that you have shown us in Jesus Christ become so conscious in our lives that we are enabled to love others in your name, and be caught up together in heavenly rapture. For yours is the kingdom forever and ever, and we are your servants in Christ Jesus our Lord. Amen.

9

O Lord, our Shepherd, who leads us by still waters and into green pastures, we thank you for the times in our lives when life is strong and good and affirming and everything seems to happen for the best. We are grateful for love and health and happiness, and for the gift of seeing with the inward eye the joys of human existence. Teach us to remember, though, that you are with us at all times, even when the waters are not still and the pastures are not green, when the way is fraught with danger or difficulty and we eat our bread in the presence of our enemies. Your lovingkindness surpasses all our imagination, and your faithfulness is to all generations. Help us to recall this in moments of adversity or disappointment, that misfortune may but strengthen our sense of your presence and encourage us in the way of wisdom. Give faith to our children, that they may learn to walk with you in the valley of the shadow of death and not be afraid of the evil. Let the mercy and goodness with which you have filled our cups overflow from us to our neighbors, that the bounty we have experienced at your hand may be theirs as well, and together we may follow you into the kingdom of faith, hope, and love forever and ever. Through Christ our Redeemer. Amen.

10

O God, who made the stars of the heavens and set the galaxies in their places, who presides over jungles and deserts and rolling oceans, it is sometimes hard for us to conceive how you can be our loving parent, infinitely concerned about the most finite things in our lives. Yet Christ has promised that not a sparrow falls without your notice, and not a child enters the world without your care. Therefore we are bold to speak before you the deepest concerns of our hearts—the illness in our bodies, the fears and loneliness of our minds, the failure of our resolve, the inadequacy of our vision, the weariness and brokenness of our relationships. Bless the child who worries about parents, the parents who worry about children. Touch those in sickrooms and hospitals with healing. Give strength to those in positions of support and ministry. Send illumination on those who are confused. Encourage the downhearted. Protect travelers. Bestow peace on those whose lives are disrupted by grief or war or other distress. Take us—who we are and what we have—for the relief of the poor and hungry of the world. And let the spirit that ruled our Lord Jesus Christ, compelling him to become an adversary to the evil powers entrenched in his world and finally to die for the sins of others, come upon us as well, that we may glorify you in the way we live and die and enter upon the life to come. For your name's sake. Amen.

11

Whenever we wait before you like this, O Lord, we become aware of two things. One is the suffering of those around us in the world; there is much grief and hurt and pain, much illness and loneliness and uncertainty. The other thing is the peace and wholeness and joy of being in your presence as we are right now. We would like to see the two brought together, so that your peace and wholeness overcome the wretchedness of people's grief and hurt and illness. Therefore we pray as your ancient people did, "Come, Lord Jesus." Come with power to bind up our wounds and heal our brokenness. Come with peace and fullness to banish envy and fear and selfish ambitions. Come with vision to make us all the family of God, eradicating hunger and poverty and estrangement and war. Lead us into the blessedness of the kingdom where still waters and a little pasture are contentment to us all, and where you are truly the center of life forever and ever. For yours are the power and the glory and the life everlasting. Amen.

12

How many times in your earthly ministry, O Lord, did you touch the fevered brows of those who were ill or the trembling hands of those who were afraid or the sagging shoulders of those bowed down by grief? Walk among us now, we pray, and touch us for the same reasons. Let those who are ill in body or in spirit feel the electricity of your presence and sense that healing is taking place. Give those who are constricted by fears and anxieties a feeling of relaxation in your grace. Let peace flow over them like a river, carrying them away from self-preoccupation and into the openness of love and sharing. Grant that the excitement of your resurrection may come upon those who sorrow, that they may walk the Emmaus Road with you and feel their hearts strangely and wonderfully warmed. We are only children, O Lord, and we often recoil from those things that should not frighten or upset us in the world. Comfort us with your presence, and teach us so to live within the disciplines of faith that we are never without you. For yours is the kingdom of light and hope and joy. Amen.

13

Almighty God, whose Spirit is in this place like dew on summer grass, like perfume in the air we breathe, like something whole and well that has just entered a sickroom, we wait before you for the touch of your hand upon us. Touch the brow that is furrowed by anxiety and make it smooth. Touch the heart that is troubled by loneliness and make it full. Touch the body that is broken by illness or exhaustion and make it whole. Touch the spirit that is hungry for your presence and make it joyful. Touch all of us with a new awareness of life, and of each other, and of your being here in our midst. Help us to put aside all thoughts and worries that hinder your presence, and relax and know that you are here, as real as the pews we sit on or the people who breathe beside us. Take away the sin that has troubled us this week, and let us feel the glory of your holiness. Make us new men and women, boys and girls, in Christ Jesus our Lord; and help us to glorify your name throughout this place and the world beyond. Amen.

14

O God of wonder and God of everyday, we thank you for both the miraculous and the ordinary in our lives: for undeserved joy and the pleasure of daily work; for sudden bursts of energy and the ability to get on from day to day; for unexpected gifts of love and the faithfulness of old relationships; for healings of the mind or body we cannot explain and the normal strength and energy we often forget we have; for vivid awareness of your presence and a quiet, undergirding sense of faith. Make us sensitive, we ask, to your working in the world around us, that we may see ourselves in a gallery of wonders every day. Teach us to see beyond the news that distresses, the remark that cuts, the disappointment in our work, the brokenness in our homes, the insufficiency of our lives, and know that you are with us, bearing our hurts and binding up our wounds in a kingdom that will be forever. Let the risen Christ reign in us until all we have is yours and all we fear is conquered. For yours is the power and the glory. Amen.

15

In the stillness, O God, come and reign over us. Help us to lift up our hearts and recognize your holy presence. Teach our wayward feet to walk in your paths once more. Restore us to the joy of your salvation and our lives to useful service in your kingdom. We hold before you today all secular authorities and rulers, that they may act righteously; all who are afflicted by grief, that their heaviness of spirit may be lightened; all who suffer from illness or injury, that they may be made whole; all who are dying of hunger, that they may be fed; all who are victims of injustice, that they may be vindicated; all who teach, that they may be wise; all who learn, that they may be well instructed; all who experience rejection or humiliation of any kind, that they may know love; and all who wait upon your kingdom's coming, that they may be satisfied. Bless with power the reading and proclaiming of your Word, both here and elsewhere, and let the spirit of your holiness descend on all your people, who wait before you now in prayer and humility, through Jesus Christ, the author and perfecter of our faith. Amen.

16

O God in whose presence we discover ourselves more truly, we know in waiting before you now that we are weak without your Spirit dwelling in us. We know that our lives don't work right apart from you—that we become anxious and self-centered, that we idolize wealth and power and position, that our needs and desires become excessive and carry us away from the simple life to which we are called in you. We pray for your healing to take place in our lives. Draw us back into your way, and help us to surrender ourselves to your will. Touch the lives of our friends, O God, who are ill in body or in spirit. Let the power that was in Jesus and the disciples enter their beings to make them well. Anoint the spirits of our young people, who are arriving at milestones in their lives. Consecrate them to your service in the world. Save them from the cheapness and unworthiness that will seek to engulf them. Tempt them to goodness in all their deeds, and let them reflect to others the image of Christ, in whose name they were baptized. Comfort those who are hurt, distressed, and without jobs or friends; lead them by still waters and into greener pastures, for your kingdom's sake. And in all things teach us to rejoice with great joy that we should be called the children of God. Amen.

17

A Pastoral Prayer for a Sunday in Autumn

In the coolness of the morning, O God, we are aware of the changing of the seasons. In the stillness of these moments, we are aware of the changing of our lives. They too have their seasons: times of doubt and times of faith, times of weariness and times of energy, times of anxiety and times of hope, times of loneliness and times of love. Help us to accept them, God, and know they are all from you. Teach us to celebrate them as part of what it is to be human, to be finite, to be your creatures. In all of these seasons, we praise you for our lives, for our insights, for the church, and for Christ, whose death atones for our sins. Give us vision, to see the world as yours. Give us courage, to claim the world for Christ. Give us love, to accept one another as brothers and sisters. Let the healing power of the cross be upon us all today—all who are ill, all who are lonely, all who grieve, all who are anxious and afraid. And may the glory of the heavens be upon all who worship you, in the name of the Father and the Son and the Holy Ghost. Amen.

18

In the stillness, O God, receive the prayers of your people. Hear the confident voices of children who are close to your kingdom and the trembling voices of adults who fear that they are not. Comfort those whose hearts have been stricken by grief, that they may live once more with hope. Bind up the wounds of the shy and the lonely and the disappointed, that they may discover love and fulfillment. Teach us all to be at peace within ourselves, that we may become peacemakers to others. Forgive us for the selfishness and shortsightedness that have blinded us to your appearances all around us—in the song of a child, the touch of a friend, the smile of a stranger, the taste of bread, the benediction of a sunset. Renew your spirit of love and creation and fellowship within us, that we may help the kingdoms of this world become the kingdom of our Christ. And in everything let us dance for the grace that is in us through Jesus our Lord, who is the alpha and the omega, the beginning and the end, incarnate and sublime. Amen.

19

O God, whose love is from everlasting to everlasting, so that we were loved before we were born and are loved in this moment and will be loved when we have passed from this life into the world to come, teach us to love. Help us to live each day with wonder, sensitive to the beauties of earth and sky, amazed at the depth and complexity of people around us, and awed by the grace of all our relationships. Secure in the compassion of Christ, let us reach out to others with our hands, our hearts, and our possessions. Show us life unfolding like a flower, full of tenderness, beauty, and gift. Take away our fear, our hesitance, our awkwardness at responding, and lead us to relax in the confidence that this is your world, and you are bringing your kingdom within it. Teach us to submit our needs to you each day and to ask for no more than we truly require. Make us bearers of peace and reconciliation, that the world may be yours through us. For yours is the love that redeems us all, through Jesus Christ. Amen.

20

In the midst of life, O God, we are also in death. Even as the green grass of summer stands tall and defiant around us, we witness the evidences of its future dying and decay. In the very hour of happiness, we are aware of a sweet sadness stealing upon us. In the moment of victory, we taste the beginnings of defeat. All life is a mixture of light and dark, ease and difficulty, joy and distress. We pray especially today for those who now experience its darker side: those who grieve at the passing of loved ones, those who struggle with great personal problems, those who feel alone or neglected, those whose lives are touched by illness or despair, those who are hungry or tired or scared. We suffer with them, O God, and ask your mercy for them. Remind them by your Holy Spirit, we pray, of the life that is ours together in Jesus Christ; let the hope that comes from him infuse them with new strength and courage and love. Save us all from bitterness and cynicism. Give us rest in your peace and fellowship in one another, and let the word of joy that is in the gospel ring in our ears with new truth and fervor this day. Through Jesus Christ our Lord. Amen.

21

O God, who knows the hearts of all and discerns the hidden secrets of our minds, you know supremely the reasons for our being here and feeling as we do today. You see the pain of the person who is tired and broken by life's disappointments—by never having had the right job or the right home or the right relationships. You acknowledge the heartache of the widow who misses her husband of fifty years or the divorced person who must now cope with life alone. You recognize the hunger of the young person for love and affection, for someone to help against the coldness and difficulty of the world. You sympathize with the agony of a parent whose beloved child has rebelled against a careful upbringing and is now living in wildness of spirit and lack of self-control. You speak to the one whose thirst is for spiritual meaning, who in the midst of a world of siren voices and selfish concerns yearns for the world of your kingdom, where all life revolves around your throne. Only you, O God, can minister to all these needs and the hundreds of others represented in this room. You alone have the words of life. Enable us to be so open to you that we can be helped this morning. Let us surrender control of ourselves and relax into the control of your Holy Spirit. Be God in our midst. Take who we are and use us in your kingdom's service. Let your love and blessing flow through us to all other persons—our family members, our neighbors, the leaders of the nations, the poor and needy of all lands—and we shall be loved and blessed in the process. For we are your people and the sheep of your pasture, through Jesus Christ our Lord. Amen.

22
A Pastoral Prayer for a Sunday in Autumn

O God, whose grace is known to us in the beauty of this autumnal morning, when the mists from the rivers rise in the cool air and the leaves of the dogwood trees are turning crimson, we thank you for the other evidences of your grace as well: for the smell of coffee perking in the kitchen; for the taste of fresh milk; for the smiles of children and the sounds of scampering feet; for the voices of loved ones and the embraces of friends; for the spires of churches and the singing of hymns; for the feel of a Bible richly bound in leather; for the words on its pages, springing to life in the imagination; for the font and the table, the twin pillars of our worship; and for all the saints, living and dead, who congregate around us at this moment to praise you for your holiness and your love and your salvation. We adore you, O God, for all your gifts and beseech you to hear our prayers for those in pain or need. Incline our hearts to you and let us walk in your way. Teach us to live together in love that we may not perish separately in hate. And let your holy will settle upon our entire world as the blue sky bends upon the earth from shore to shore and pole to pole. Through Jesus Christ our Lord. Amen.

23

We are the little folk, O God, lost in the cogs and wheels of the great world, trampled by circumstances, befuddled by the events of our times. We feel put upon, neglected, used, and discarded. Our sense of self-worth is very small and our confidence in ourselves is nothing to brag about. Even our sin is not distinguished in our own minds, and we hesitate to trouble you about it. What we need in life is to start over, to begin at the beginning again and have a clear sense of purpose, to know how to use who we are and what we have to the best advantage. We need to feel that we belong and that we matter, both to ourselves and to other people. We need to know that life is good and that every day has meaning. We need to feel fresh and vital and happy and useful. In short, O God, we need to be born again, to be born from above, the way Jesus described it to Nicodemus. We need to start anew today and be able to walk off from our old lives and failures as if they didn't exist. We need to feel like totally new creatures in your love and purpose for us. Help us do it, dear God; give us the grace and the courage to leave behind our pessimism and gloom and self-despising and to walk off into a new future with you. Show us how to forget the things that are past and to reach forward to life in Christ Jesus. Make us into your triumphant people, whose gift for life is that we even love and respect ourselves. And let your kingdom come through us, today and forever. Through Christ our Lord. Amen.

24

O God, who has given us the earth and filled it with every sort of good thing, and has set us in it as enjoyers and caretakers, celebrators and stewards, we raise our prayer of thanksgiving for life and beauty and grace. There is nothing necessary to our peace and fulfillment that you have not provided. Yet in ignorance and pride and willfulness we have often squandered your gifts and missed the way to more abundant living. As we confess our wrongdoing, mend our hearts with your forgiveness and restore us in the way. Teach us to pause each day to see what you have made that is new and fresh and gracious in our world and to live with thankful attitudes. Touch with your healing those who are ill or stricken in body. Embrace with your gentle care those who suffer loneliness or disappointment or betrayal or resentment. Bring fruitfulness and progress to the lives of people in developing nations. Grant to our leaders the hearts and vision of giants, that they may plan wisely and bravely for generations yet unborn. Let all of us who are in this place bury our envy, prejudice, and selfishness, and receive the benediction of your Spirit, who leads us to peace and love and gentleness with all others. Through Jesus Christ our Lord. Amen.

25

O God, who has ordained the seasons of the year and also the seasons of our lives, we praise you for the steadfastness of your love and mercy, which support us in every season and time of life. Help us now to open ourselves to the gift of your presence, which will transform our very existence. Where there is fear, give courage; where there is anxiety, give peace; where there is loneliness, give companionship. Let the mind of your Son Jesus become our mind as well, drawing us into fellowship and commitment and service. In a world that grows daily more difficult and complicated, lead us into simplicity of heart and soul. As others contend for place and possessions, make us joyful with relationships. Where the paths that we must walk become steep and narrow or overgrown with briars and weeds, hold our hands lest we stumble. Reveal yourself especially to those who suffer grief or illness, that they may be encouraged by a deeper knowledge of you. Help us to hear your Word for each of us as we wait before you in reverence and love. Through Jesus Christ. Amen.

26

A Pastoral Prayer for Children and Young People

God of the small and the great, God of the young and the old, we hold before you today the children and young people of the world: hollow-eyed babies who are starving to death; frightened youngsters already in military service; sickly and deformed children who will never know a normal life; battered and abused children who can never rest because of what they have experienced; children of plenty, whose only companion is a television set, so that their view of reality is distorted from the beginning; children of prejudice and ignorance, condemned to repeat their parents' lives in a hopeless cycle; children of shyness and fear, who can deal with life only in fantasy, when the doors are shut; children of divorce, who often feel confused and guilty and alone. The children are our hope, O God; they are the progeny you promised to Abraham. And somehow we have failed them. We have given them the wrong world, shown them the wrong goals, burdened them with the wrong ambitions. Save the children, O God. Help them to know your great love for them. Heal their broken minds and bodies. Show them how to be pure and good and caring. Redeem them from bad beginnings, from poor self-images, from attachment to drugs and alcohol, from wasteful sexuality, from resentment and rebellion. Lead them in the paths of righteousness, for your name's sake. Fill their cups to overflowing. Let them rejoice in your lovingkindness and follow in the way that leads to eternal life. And grant to us all a sense of what it means to be family and community together, that we may truly be the people of God. Through Jesus Christ our Lord. Amen.

27

We confess, O God, that there are many gifts we receive each day without thanksgiving: the hug of a child, the song of a bird at the eave of the house, a small, cool breeze in the heat of the day, a night without restlessness, a call from a friend, the sound of laughter on a playground, the thrill and entertainment of a good book, the taste of fresh berries, the memory of a happy time, the promise of our faith. Here, where we sing the songs of Zion and hear the reading of your Word, we are reminded that every good and perfect gift comes from you, and we raise our voices in gratitude for the beauty and glory of your creation. We applaud, O God, your desire and plan for justice in the world, and lift up to you now the poor and the hungry, the lonely and the broken, the outcast and the ill. Grant peace and grace in their lives, and help those of us who have gifts to share with them to stretch forth our hands this day in love and thoughtfulness. Teach our hearts to be more sensitive, that we may see Christ in the beggar and find your kingdom in our attempts to make the world a better place. Let us remember those who have lived and died in the faith before us and be joined to them in spirit as we praise and magnify your name, through Jesus Christ. Amen.

28

O God, who out of your own will and purpose did choose to create the world and to love those who inhabit it, and who in the fullness of time did send your only begotten Son among us to instruct us and to die for our sins, there is nothing we can do for you or for those around us that is not merely a response to your goodness and faithfulness to us. We confess that we often live on the surface of life, without contemplating our debts and obligations. We take without thought of giving; we receive without intention of repaying. Forgive us for this shallowness in our natures, and help us to live more thoughtfully. Build up within us an eternal perspective on life, that we may be less anxious about the smaller things—what we shall eat or wear or see at the movies—and more committed to larger things: whether there is justice in the world, so that the poor may eat and drink, and whether human relationships are daily improved, bringing us closer and closer to the community of faith in your kingdom. Give us a sober and truthful understanding of the church, that we may see it for what it is: a divine gift beyond all the local problems of gossip and personality and judgmentalism and the territorial imperative. Call us once more to participate in the church—to *be* the church—to share our means and talents and love in the fellowship of the saints, yearning for your will to be done on earth and for our spirits to be caught up in your great overmastering Spirit. Strengthen the leaders of this and every local congregation. Impart clarity and effectiveness to the preaching of your Word. Let the gospel be heard so completely and compellingly in our midst that we shall fall in love with it all over again and become followers of Christ who sing in the way and shower gifts of healing and unity upon all who live in the shadow of our passing. Save us from small passions and futile expenditure of energy, and direct us into channels of power and effectiveness. And regenerate in us today the sense of Christ's call and commission that will lift our hearts and reclaim our imaginations, renewing this church and its mission to the world. Through him who lives forevermore and reigns with you and the Holy Spirit, world without end. Amen.

29

O God, whose breath is like the dawn of a new day and whose arms are like the great rocks that support the land and the sea, we bow our heads to make a double confession: of the sinfulness of our natures and of the hope we have in your name. You have shown us in Christ how far from the mark of love and sincerity we often stray, and yet you have also shown us in him the depth of your compassion for us and the way we can be saved. Let your Holy Spirit come upon us now in power and tenderness, drawing us back into the way of righteousness. Heal those who are sick. Lift the hearts of those who are depressed. Point the way for those who are confused. Embrace those who are lonely and afraid. Convict those who feel no need for repentance. Enlist those who are not now serving their fellow human beings. Support those who grieve for lost homes, lost positions, lost times, and lost loved ones. Show us how to be loving and gentle and generous with all you have given us, peacemakers in a world that is all but devoid of peace. Help us to savor small moments and beautiful thoughts, and to speak your name softly in the night, for it is a name above every name in both heaven and earth, and worthy to be adored in this life and the next. And grant us your peace, through Christ our Savior. Amen.

30

Give us unity of heart as we pray, O God, that we may pray as one with you and one with each other and one within ourselves. Let your Holy Spirit cover us and bind us and draw us close together, that we may be whole within our minds. Save us from caring about small things that do not matter in the light of your eternity, and help us to pray for things of everlasting consequence. We beseech you for the salvation of the nations and for your peace to descend upon us. Strengthen all bearers of your Word this day, whether lay or clergy, that it may go forth in power to convict of sin and turn people's eyes upon you. Let Christ be lifted over the earth as a sign of your love and reconciliation, and let us all cry out at once for our redemption. Send justice among the poor and ignorant and diseased of every nation, that the hungry may be fed and the lowly exalted. Grant mercy to us who have so much and share so little, who seem to think we are owed what we have and do not hold it in trust from you. Send conversion upon our spirits, that we may be humbled and have compassion and reach out to a needy, dying world. Grant comfort to those who mourn, that their spirits may be refreshed in remembering your Word and your salvation, which are established forever and ever despite the ravages of age and accident. Enable us to walk in Christ among the young, that they may be drawn into his yoke while there is time for them and time for the world.

Give the peace of your presence to all who dream dark dreams or live in fear and anxiety. And help us to communicate freely with one another, accepting one another in love and compassion as we have been accepted in Christ. For yours is the kingdom beyond all our little kingdoms and the joy beyond all our sorrow. Amen.

31

O God, whose grace is like a canopy of love spread over our lives, we thank you for the banquet spirit of the kingdom, in which are gathered all the colors of life and all the peoples of the world. We celebrate today the gospel of your Son, in whom we have our redemption and the ongoing transformation of our hearts and minds. Save us, we pray, from routine ailments and duties, and reveal to us the rich, exciting possibilities for a future in which we exalt the poor and embrace our enemies. Show us the way beyond our dreams and the vague agreement that our lives should be lived for your kingdom's glory to specific realities that involve us in carrying out your will. Teach us how to fill our cups with cool water and reach out to thirsty persons. Show us the joy of giving both our shirts and our coats to those who have none. Grant us the privilege of sharing our bread with people who are dying of hunger. Enable us not only to walk the mile that is required of us, but, finding our strength in love, to go the second mile as well. You have given us too much, dear God, to forsake us with our gifts. Make us a servant people, eager to draw others beneath the canopy of grace and into the banquet hall of the Spirit. Touch now the fevered brow, the broken body, the distraught mind. Lead those who are confused or discouraged into new, green pastures of the soul. And bind our hearts in the fellowship of a shared vision as we sing your praises and wait before you in the gentleness of expectation. For your name's sake. Amen.

32

O God of all mercies, we celebrate in your presence the advances of life in our nation: that with the exception of the HIV virus there are no great and deadly plagues sweeping across the world as they once did; that few children die of diseases and few women of childbirth; that people live with renewed hearts and replaced organs; that there are medicines for treating afflictions of the mind; that there are stockpiles of grain to offset the years of drought; that there is heat and light in even the poorest homes; that there are knowledge of sanitation and provisions for general health; that there are retirement plans and insurance and supervision of the economy. We live in a day that our grandfathers and grandmothers only dreamed about. Yet, O God, there are many things lacking in our way of life. We have not learned to love one another as we should, or to raise our children with respect for your name. We still become envious and proud and resentful. We still live in fear and anxiety and brokenness. You have helped us to conquer most of the physical problems, dear God. Now help us to conquer the emotional and spiritual problems as well by surrendering our wills to yours and allowing you to mold us in the image of your Son Jesus, who has shown us the way to a new and higher humanity. For your name's sake. Amen.

33

O God, whose love is steadfast and whose grace is beyond all measure, prove yourself shockingly in our midst. Move upon our minds and hearts with such incontrovertible presence that we may not mistake it for the flutterings of our own self-consciousness. Arrest our attention as you arrested that of Moses at the burning bush. Excite our interest as you excited that of Isaiah in the temple. Overcome our lethargy as you overcame that of the disciples on the Mount of Transfiguration. Become the reality you are—for *us*—that all other realities may retreat into shadowy paleness beside you. Expose our sin, quicken our commitment, stir up our love and concern, call us into your service. Help us to be done with lesser things—with anxieties about health or worldly success, with devotion to trivial goals, with pursuit of immoral ends—and, clinging to Christ, aim only to hear your voice and obey your will. Transform this church, with all its mighty potential, into a lighthouse for the unredeemed and a courthouse for the unsatisfied and a warehouse for the unfed and unclothed. Comfort those who grieve; heal those who languish; and give wisdom to those who vote. Restore our nation to the level of sanity and devotion it knew in its finest hours. Be God in our midst, and let us fall down before you as your people to cry out in joy and thanksgiving, worshiping you with all the saints and angels now and forever. Amen.

34

O God, who watches over us in the restlessness of the night and whose arms are around us when we feel most alone and unworthy, teach us how to live with the special feeling of grace abounding. Open our hearts to know your transforming love. Help us to feel good about ourselves—that because we are loved by you we are acceptable to significant other persons in our lives. Heal our inner spirits of self-doubt and fear and anxiety. Lead us to a sense of wholeness and belonging, of living in a world of goodness and beauty that is filled with the potential for wonderful relationships and personal joy. Bless our children with feelings of warmth and love, that they may grow to maturity with the ability to care for others, knowing always that you care for them. Let the fellowship of this congregation be the matrix in which people come to trust and understand one another and find forgiveness for all past failures. May the spirit of Christ be so strong and lively in our midst that to spend an hour here is to feel ourselves irradiated by love and hope and joy. In the mystery of your creation, O God, we would even ask, within the boundaries of your will, for the healing of our bodies, and not of ours only, but of those within the radius of our voices and our love. There is so much you want to give us, and so little we have been able to accept. Open us, O God; teach us; and then use us to bless your world. Through Jesus Christ our Lord. Amen.

35

Minister now, O God, to our weaknesses: to the needs of our bodies, which are many and varied; to loneliness, which fills us with self-pity; to fears and anxieties, which paralyze us against useful action; to jealousies, which blind us to the abundant riches of our own lives; to anger and resentment, which choke out sweetness and grace in our minds; to selfishness, which limits our interaction with the world, whereby we might receive much more than we do; to slothfulness and lack of discipline, which fills us with feelings of guilt and ineffectiveness; to littleness of spirit, which restricts us from joyful participation in this community and from discoveries that would sweep us away from the dullness and boredom of ourselves and into the excitement of your kingdom that is continually coming in our midst. Grant that in the company of like-minded souls we may even now be persuaded by the gospel to abandon our grasp on those things that hinder our full conversion to Christ, and to sail freely into new seas of the spirit where life is deeper and richer and more filled with meaning. Restore wonder to our eyes and love to our hearts. Receive us into the mystery of your presence and transform us into servants of your grace. Through him who knew you perfectly and could not be tempted to betray what he knew so well. Amen.

36

O God, whose love is more than we can ever know, like that of a parent who lies awake at night worrying about a child that has not come home, we wait in silence before you, hoping to be changed. We would like to have more time and energy for the important things of life. We would like to be less concerned about ourselves and more caring toward others. We would like to be more cooperative with others at work and school, and to fit in better in groups at church and in the community. But as much as we want these things, O God, we lack the power to bring them about. Only your power can help us do them. Only when we more fully realize your love for us and know that we have received grace in your sight are we able to begin to change and live differently. Help us to know your love, O God; to remember that you have given your only Son to die for us; and to realize that his Spirit is here today, empowering us to become the sons and daughters of God, filled with joy and truth. Speak to us in the hymns and prayers and sermon; whisper to us in the moments of silence, the shafts of light through the colored glass, the tones of an anthem. And then, as sons and daughters, let us throw ourselves at your feet, desiring to be your servants. Through Jesus Christ our Lord. Amen.

37

In the stillness, O God, hear the sounds of our many voices. Some are lonely and cry for companionship. Some are hurt and ask for healing. Some are confused and seek direction. Some are compassionate and raise petitions for others. Some are merely glad to be here, and express their joy. Some don't know why they have come or what to say to you in a time like this. Gather us all up, with our many voices, into a sense of your holy presence. Transform us into the body of Christ—into a living, breathing organism. Let the health of those who are healthy flow into the lives of those who are not. Let the Spirit of love and caring come upon us, transforming us from limited, self-centered individuals into channels of your blessing and energy in the world. Take control of our hearts and minds. Bend us from thoughts of striving and gaining to attitudes of sharing and giving. Make us sensitive to one another's needs and feelings. Help us to embrace the world of the poor and neglected, even becoming like them in order to serve them. Create a new atmosphere among us for living in the image of your Son, that we may be thankful and responsive creatures. And as we turn from stillness to praise, may the stillness remain inside us and go with us always. Through Jesus Christ, the giver of peace, to whom be glory forever and ever. Amen.

38

Dear God, in whose almighty plan there are no losers except those who turn themselves from you and willfully deny the life you offer them, we thank you for the closeness we feel as a community today, for the joy of friendships, for the sense of mission in a world of need, for the beauty of children's faces upturned in worship, and for the grace of old people's hands folded in the happiness of your presence. We would pray for the nations of the world, that they may be sensible and forgiving; and for the church in all its manifestations, that it may be exemplary and redemptive; and for ourselves as followers of Christ, that we may help to bring peace and love into the world. Speak today to the lonely, O God, both here in this sanctuary and in other parts of this city, that they may lift up their hearts at your approach. Anoint the sick, the tired, and the discouraged, that they may feel your new life entering their weak hearts and bodies. Challenge the bored and apathetic, that they may create new pathways for the poor and downtrodden of the earth. Reunite the disaffected and give them the sense of contrition and humility and compassion we should all feel before the cross of our Savior. Purify us of evil or unworthy ambitions, cleanse us of ignoble thoughts, incline our wills to your desires for our lives, and make us receptive to your word, spoken in song and silence and sermon, that we may become more truly your children, whose ways are your ways and whose thoughts are your thoughts. Through him who was so perfectly united to you that he was able to say, "the Father and I are one,"* even Christ our Lord. Amen.

39

In the ups and downs of life, with good times and bad, sunny days and dark, we pray to you, O God, who are always the same, with love and forgiveness, with healing for our brokenness. We thank you for Jesus Christ and for your Holy Spirit, active in the world for the reunion of all minds and hearts into eternal oneness. Bless, we pray, every straggling attempt of people to get together in amity and goodwill: of married couples who have had disagreements and wounded feelings, of parents and children who have been offended, of friends or associates who have experienced disappointment in one another, of groups or companies or denominations or institutions that have allowed their differences to be magnified over their agreements, of nations that have dealt with one another out of pride or arrogance or selfish greed. Make us instruments of your peace, that we may help to draw others into unity and cooperation with the Spirit. Teach us not to fear rejection or disillusionment in the work of your kingdom, but to remember always the undaunted faith of our Lord Jesus upon the cross, when he asked forgiveness for the very persons who caused his pain. Give us such a sense of love and acceptance that we shall not even be afraid of death, the great divider, but know that you have conquered it by making us one with you. To that end, O God, let your Holy Spirit fall upon us all, both here in this sanctuary and wherever friends are gathered, to make us all one and to strengthen us in our weakness. Through Jesus our Redeemer. Amen.

---

* John 10:30.

40

O God of tree and flower, of child and parent, we thank you for the surpassing beauty of the world in which we live, and for the relationships of kin and kind that enhance our sense of joy. You are truly a God of wonder and of love. But there are some who are troubled in this world of flowers and love because they are looking at it with the eyes of those who know they must leave it. Comfort them, we pray, with the presence that makes all life one, both in this world and the next. Some are disturbed because they can't own the world, because ambitions are unfulfilled and desires unrequited. Help them, we ask, to discover the joy of little things, the delight of admiring, the excitement of sharing. Some are unable to see the glory of the world because they regard it from positions of poverty or hunger or imprisonment of one kind or another. Minister to their needs, we beseech you, through our means and the means of others, that we may all be joined together in praise of your name and of the world you have envisioned. Let us this day ponder the gifts that are ours at your hand, and, coming before the table where we remember the death of your Son, rededicate them to your dream for all humankind, in which there will be no more pain or hunger or personal estrangement, but only love and fellowship and peace. Through Jesus Christ our Lord. Amen.

41

O Lord for all seasons, we thank you for the springtime of life, when wonder is large and joys are daily, when hope rises with the morning sun and disappointments vanish as quickly as they are conceived. We praise you for the summer of life, when strength and beauty grow intertwined and love and fruitfulness lie heavy on the vine. We lift up our hearts for the autumn of life, when souls are mellow and more relaxed, and the glory of age rests colorfully on the bough. We incline ourselves in worship for the winter of life, when things stand stark and bare for what they really are, and the majesty of existence is exposed in all its grandeur. O Lord for all seasons, be near us in every age. Teach us to sing your praises as children and to hum your glory as old men and women. Let the strength of your hand bear us up as youths and direct us in your way when we mature. Make us servants of your Word and of your Christ. Let us draw the whole world into your service and pray for your justice among the nations. Forgive us when we falter and comfort us when we are in distress. Grant that we shall worship you with every passing breath and, when we breathe no more, shall join our songs to all of those beyond the seasons, who surround the heavenly throne. Through Jesus Christ our Lord. Amen.

42
A Pastoral Prayer for Thanksgiving

O God of cornfields and festive board, of firesides and pilgrims' dreams, we thank you today for the panorama of our faith: for ancient prophets who dared to speak for truth in a time of broken loyalties; for the humble Nazarene invested with the power of miracles and life beyond the grave; for faithful apostles who carried your Word in spite of dungeon, fire, and sword; for builders of churches and teachers of children in the long centuries between then and now; for reformers and scholars who have preserved and purified the Bible; for our fathers and mothers in the faith who laid the groundwork of our own belief, and built this church and provided for the work of the ministry in this place. We thank you for the community of followers represented here today and for the love and hope and mission that we share. Hear our prayers for the sick and sorrowing among us. Make us repentant for our sin and for the wastefulness of our lives apart from you. Teach us reverence and gratitude for the small things of life: the cheerful light of a candle, the gaiety of a child, the warmth of a fire, the refreshment of a cup of water, the joy of a friend's embrace. And above all, give us your Holy Spirit, that we may live not in ourselves but in your will and power, which are ever shaping the world to its final destiny of peace and fruitfulness, through Jesus Christ our Lord. Amen.

43
A Pastoral Prayer for Advent

O Lord, whose presence alone makes Christmas and without whom all our efforts at joy are doomed to failure, we wait before you now as those who have dwelled in darkness but have caught a glimpse of a great light. Help us follow the narrow visions we have had until they lead us to the fullness of your love and mercy. Let the song of the angels at Bethlehem be heard once more in our hearts, that our faith may be renewed and our commitment rekindled. Fill us with compassion for one another—for children bright with wonder, for widows and widowers saddened by memories of loved ones, for the sick and the tired and the broken, for peoples of the world struggling for life and livelihood and education. Show us how to share our strength and peace with them as you have shared yours with us. And grant that our meeting with you today may inspire us to new ways of relating to one another and more wholesome ways of going about our work and our business. Through him whose coming has changed the world. Amen.

44
A Pastoral Prayer for Advent

O God most high, who made yourself visible in a child lying in a manger and a man dying on a cross, and who can now be seen in churches decorated for Christmas and banks of children singing carols, help us to see you in other places as well: in the faces of the tired and the poor as they long for help; in schoolrooms and theaters; in the efforts of legislators to raise the standards of living; in the attempts of world leaders to avoid war; in the frenzy of shoppers to find gifts for friends and loved ones; in the weariness of store clerks; in the labor of those who cook and clean and wait upon others; in the expectancy of children; in the tenderness of parents; in the patience of doctors and nurses; in the grace with which people die. Forgive us for self-centeredness, for overwork and exhaustion, and for failure to expect you or to see you in all these places and many more. Teach us the art of watching for you, of being present when you are present, of caring for the world as you care. Make time our friend instead of our enemy. Slow us down for feeling and being. Fill us with your Spirit. As you came into a cattle stall so many years ago, come now into the humble dwellings of our hearts and fit us for lives of service. Through him whom angels sang and shepherds adored, even Christ our Savior. Amen.

45
A Pastoral Prayer for Advent

O God, whose presence is felt in advent wreaths and Christmas lights and the sweet perfume of fir trees, grant to us a sense of your reality that extends far beyond these, into the harder and more conflictual areas of life—into the room where a patient is dying of cancer, into the marketplace where corporations struggle for supremacy, into parts of the world where wars are being fought, into hearts that are trying to cope with loss and addiction and depression and boredom and loneliness. Let your coming into the world be more than an excuse for an annual excursion into sentimentality and romanticism. Let it be a true incarnation, by which we see you enmeshed in all the problems and difficulties of our human flesh, in order that we may hear the gospel of resurrection and victory with something approximating the real hope and joy it carries. Speak to us of stables and mangers, but speak to us also of the part you bear in the politics and economics of the world. Speak to us of shepherds and angels' choirs, but speak to us as well of your role in medicine and psychiatry and education and philanthropy. Speak to us of stars and visiting wise men; but speak to us too of your struggle against both personal and corporate injustice, your concern for individuals and races, your place in the way we live and love and worship. Transform us from being casual followers who don't really know Christ into true followers who not only know him but will follow him to the death. Turn us from being so everlastingly concerned about ourselves into those who love your world with a passion and will lay down their lives for your little ones. And then Christmas will really become the Mass of our Christ, and we shall sing your praises forever and ever. Amen.

46
A Pastoral Prayer for Advent

Come, Lord Jesus, into lives being prepared for your service like halls that are swept and dusted and decorated for Christmas. Come, Lord Jesus, into a church that is waiting for your coming, that longs for transformation, that yearns to be church as the disciples became church in the early days of our history. Come, Lord Jesus, among families that will give you a home and celebrate your advent not once a year but every day. Come, Lord Jesus, among men and women who work in the marketplace and who will carry you there as on a portable throne, lifting you high so that everyone may see and worship you. Come, Lord Jesus, among students who will value your companionship in the classroom and on the campus and who will honor your high moral claims on their lives as well as on their minds. Come, Lord Jesus, among ministers and boards of elders and deacons who would bow down to you and confess your leadership in all their activities. Come, Lord Jesus, among casual churchgoers who would be casual no more but would sing of your power over death and your power over their lives. Come, Lord Jesus, among the sick and over-borne, who would welcome your healing presence and live gratefully in your service. Come, Lord Jesus, among the poor and neglected peoples of the world, who would be poor no more if once you visited them. Come, Lord Jesus, your servants wait and sing your advent here. For you are the Lord of all! Amen.

47

A Pastoral Prayer for Advent

O Lord, whose coming into the world has produced such wonderful changes—evolving the church, converting governments, and transforming human life—we bow before you now at the beginning of another advent season. Do we dare to hope, O Lord, that there may be great changes in our lives during these weeks? That those whose hearts are heavy may find relief? That those who walk in the darkness of confusion may see light dawning before them? That those who are angry may find it possible to love and forgive? That those who face hard decisions may be given courage and clarity of mind? That those who communicate poorly may learn to embrace and be embraced? That those who are shy and withdrawn may learn the joy of easy relationships? We do not deplore our humanity, O Lord, for you have accepted that. You came among us in the form of a child and grew to manhood in a normal family, and dealt with daily life as we must deal with it, and suffered rejection and torture and humiliation and death as we also suffer them. We do not ask that we may be less human but that we may be more human, that we may find the deep centers within ourselves where love and compassion and strength abide, and operate from them instead of from the whims and ambitions and lusts and jealousies that stir us on the surface of life. We remember many others to whom we hope you will come in this advent time: the prisoners of the world, who languish in places of cruelty and inhumanity; those who hunger, both in this nation and abroad; alcoholics and smokers and drug addicts, who lack the mastery of their own bodies; AIDS and cancer victims, who face untimely deaths; illiterate persons, who live in a bondage we cannot understand; children who are abused by their parents or teachers or other children; persons accused of crimes they did not commit; persons living with crimes they did commit; people who cannot cope with ordinary affairs and so become dysfunctional in one way or another. This world is either heaven or hell, O Lord, depending on whether you are with us or not. Do come to us during these days of advent, and to all others as well. Let the world be redeemed by your loving presence, that the kingdoms we have known may become the kingdom of our Christ and that your name may be glorified forever. Amen.

48

A Pastoral Prayer for Advent

O God of wreaths and bows, of trees and candlelight, of family reunions and festive dinners, we remember that you are also God of the hungry and the hurting, of the outcasts and the homeless, of the angry and the ill-favored. Forgive us if we like to imagine you in the more pleasant aspects of our lives and remind us that when we are in need we want you on our side. Help us in all the rush and busyness of this season not to forget that Christ came for the sake of the poor and oppressed, and to take time to meditate on what this means to the way we live and behave toward one another. Make us sensitive to the overworked and under-paid people around us, to those who will spend Christmas on the streets, to the residents of retirement homes, to patients in the hospitals, to shoppers and clerks and people in the stores, to the thousands of people worldwide who have lost loved ones in recent days, and to the many in our own midst who are tired or lonely or out of work or facing the holidays without people for whom they have cared. Show us that the pain of Christmas is not heavy to bear because you bear it with us. Lead us through the pain to the insight and joy of Christmas. Let us truly know what this time is about, and then let us fall on our knees to worship. We remember in our prayers the leaders of our nation, and of other nations, that they may be drawn closer to you and your will for the world. Let the star that guided wise men to the Child in Bethlehem beckon us all to a new age of understanding and peace, when love will put an end to war and hatred and prejudice, and when your name will cause rejoicing in all the streets and ghettos of all the cities of the earth. Through him whose birth began the new age. Amen.

49

A Pastoral Prayer for Advent

God of love and God of joy, God of Bethlehem's baby boy, we bow before you in this season of goodwill to thank you for the goodwill you have shown to us. We do not deserve the gifts that enrich our lives, yet they continue to come. Teach us to live in sensitivity and awareness, that we may know each one of them and respond with grateful hearts. Forgive us for the anxieties that choke our existence, and help us to be free and happy. As you have entered our lives through a lowly cattle stall, make us ready to enter the lives of others through the humblest of offices. Take away our false pride and sense of self-importance, that we may live openly toward others and relate to them on the basis of care and compassion. Let the star that led the wise men to the King of Kings shine in our hearts and imaginations this Christmas and lead us to worship him where he may be found, in the hovels of the poor, at the tables of the hungry, at the bedsides of the sick, in the excited faces of little children. Comfort those who mourn, heal those who are ill, and mend the lives of those who are broken. Give us yourself for heavenly food, and let us be your children in the world. For yours is the kingdom of eternal light and joy. Amen.

50
A Pastoral Prayer for Christmas

O God of stars and stables, God of angels and shepherds, we celebrate your name for the gift of the Christ Child and sing your praises for your humbly dwelling among men and women of the world. Give us hearts filled with your presence, that we may be changed from children of darkness into children of light. Teach our tongues to speak of your greatness, that all our households may reflect your glory. Bring hope and love and joy into our midst, that we may share with all the world the faith that moves mountains and the belief that banishes sorrow. Anoint our sick with the confidence that says, "Whether I live or whether I die, I am the Lord's." Surround our children with care and protection, that they may grow up in grace and goodness. Show us how to live in peace and fullness with one another, sharing what we have with the poor and the humble. Enable us to give, as you did, without assessing the worthiness of the receiver, and to love, as you did, without counting the cost. And amid all the holly and the candles and the sweet smell of cedar, let us give thanks with all our hearts for the real message of Christmas, that you have come among us today in order that we may live with you forever. Through the One who was born at Bethlehem, Jesus our Redeemer. Amen.

51
A Pastoral Prayer for Christmas

O God, whose power was revealed in the creation of the world and whose love was made known in the child born in a stable, we hold up before you today a world broken and bleeding and starving and dying. We remember the embattled peoples of distant nations, and the starving infants of Africa and India, and the despairing prisoners in thousands of jails, and the poor and distressed and lonely people in our own neighborhoods and communities. Everywhere people are crying "Peace, peace," and there is no peace. We pray for your peace, O Holy One, the peace that passes all human understanding. Let it come into our hearts and minds and transform us into people of peace and goodwill. Let it make us ambassadors for Christ in all the world, sending the good news of your kingdom and gifts of medicine and education and food and technology around the globe. Forgive us for our years of selfishness and blindness and inactivity. Convert us and this church into a first-aid station for life's walking wounded. Teach us to love one another until there is no hate or jealousy or resentment among us. Touch us with the healing power of your Holy Spirit, that miracles of love, forgiveness, and redemption may occur in our midst. Show us the way of your Son and help us to walk in it. Let the glory of eternal life begin to flower in our lives here and now, changing us into the saints we shall become and witnessing through our attitudes and behavior to the One who reigns with you forever and ever. Amen.

52
A Pastoral Prayer for Christmas

In a world of cold and hunger and terror, O God, there is still room for the star of Christmas to shine. We remember our brothers and sisters in destitute nations and our brothers and sisters who are destitute in this nation. We pray for those whose lives are fraught with fear and hardship and disease, who are rarely free from pain and worry. We lift up all prisoners, all teachers, all ministers, all doctors and nurses and social workers, all legislators and lawyers and judges. We intercede for students and dreamers and reformers, for farmers and laborers and factory owners, for mothers and fathers and children. In short, O God, we recognize that everyone in all the earth needs your loving, redemptive mercy and that we ourselves are no exception. Pour out your grace once more upon your people. Let the gift of Christmas joy be ours again. Stir us from lethargy and apathy and resignation. Send the star to shine on us in our moods of depression and unbelief and to lead us afresh to the embodiment of your love in the Child of Bethlehem. Let all of life stop for us, as it did for the shepherds and wise men, and let us adore your Christ. Then send us forth as they went, proclaiming good news to the nations and singing your praises, for you have shown us a glimpse of your kingdom of love and light. Amen.

53

A Pastoral Prayer for Christmas

O God, whose throne of grace is hymned with continual praise and thanksgiving, we add our voices to those of all the saints and angels and say, "Thank you, Lord, for your love and mercy and power that flow constantly into our universe, filling it with hope and energy and redemption!" There is nothing in us that deserves your gifts, and yet you have chosen to share yourself with the very least of us and to send your bounty upon us even when our hearts were not turned in your direction. Help us in recognition and gratitude to turn our thoughts and lives to you and to align ourselves with your hopes and vision for our world. Use us as instruments for loving your little ones in all the earth—for seeing that they are fed and clothed and educated, that they receive the medical and technical aid they need, and that with all of this, they hear the good news of your kingdom in Jesus Christ. Bless with your mercy in this holiday season all children who are away from home, all students who travel on the highways, all the elderly who languish in pain or loneliness, all patients in hospitals, all inmates in prisons, all ministers and teachers of the gospel, and all servants of society. Let the hope that was born at the coming of Christ continue to flower among us, leading us to new heights of commitment and new depths of love for one another. For yours are the kingdom and the power and the glory forever. Amen.

54
A Pastoral Prayer for Christmas

O Lord of Christmas, whose breath is mercy and whose arms are grace, we crowd before you as the lost, the tired, the confused, and the amazed. Still the fluttering of our hearts with your divine calmness, and touch our eyes until they see your advent here. Teach us to be simple and good in our lives, affecting only those things that make for love and joy and peace among us. Help us to share our bread with the hungry of the world and our hearts with the lonely. Let the glitter of tinsel and the light from our candles be dim beside the glow of our happiness in Christ. Draw us once more on that ancient pilgrimage to Bethlehem and permit us to stand in awe before the sight that made angels sing and kings produce their treasures. Grant that the peace that passes all human understanding may settle upon the nations of the world, until shepherds watching their flocks by night are more important than satellites watching Washington and Moscow and Beijing. Turn us into the way of the Messiah, that we may prefer justice and love to power and wealth.

Show us the beauty of a star and the innocence of a maid and the simplicity of a stable and the glory of a Child, that we may be reclaimed from all our errant ways and reborn in the spirit of Christmas. For your name's sake. Amen.

55
A Pastoral Prayer for Christmas Eve

In the stillness of the night, O Lord, our Christ was born. In the stillness of this night, let him come again. Let the voice that calmed the sea calm all our fears and anxieties. Let the hands that healed the lepers heal our infirmities of mind and body. Let the eyes that saw the world always from the viewpoint of eternity help us to see that way too. Let the arms that were always there to console and support the poor and unfortunate be around us as well. We know we have made little room for him, that our lives have been busy and self-centered and preoccupied. But help us now to clear a space for him that will always be his, and from that space let him reorder our time and our affections and our commitments. We pray for our weary world: for all who have endured disasters of one kind or another; for those who languish in prison; for all who suffer injustice and repression by their governments; for all who are abused in their own households, either physically or emotionally; for all who are thanklessly overworked or needlessly under-employed; for all who struggle with disabilities or carry burdens not shared by others; for all who cannot read; for all who live in substandard housing or are homeless on the streets and roadsides of the world. May the Savior of the world take pity on them. May your kingdom swiftly come, redeeming the human situation. May we become the instruments of your peace and mediators of your grace, O Lord of Christmas, O God of all the ages. Even so, come, Lord Jesus, and forgive our sins. Come, Lord Jesus, and give power to your truth. Come, Lord Jesus, and lead us to heaven. Amen.

56

A Pastoral Prayer for Christmas Day

The bells ring out, O God, the best news mortal ears have ever heard, that Jesus Christ is born! How different our lives would be if we did not know, imprisoned in ignorance and superstition and hopelessness. How different our world would be if he had not come, utterly lost in greed and self-ishness and cynicism. Yet our lives have not been different enough, and our world has not been different enough, because we have not sufficiently communicated to others the wonderful news of his coming and have not completely surrendered to it ourselves. Let it be your Christmas gift to us this day that we shall understand and surrender and become so filled with joy that we shall find ways of sharing our faith with the world around us. We hold before you today all our problems and sorrows, that they may become offerings to the Christ Child; all our friends and visitors, that they may receive an extraordinary blessing from being here; all of those who travel, that they may be kept in safety; all of those who must work today—guards, police officers, fire fighters, nurses, doctors, telephone operators, engineers, and people in other forms of service—that they may some-how be visited by a special sense of your presence; all who are kept from home by military duty or for other reasons, that they may be aware of sharing in the divine love; all the poor and homeless, that they may yet keep Christmas in their hearts; all the leaders of states and nations, that they may remember the sacredness of their trust and receive power to fulfill it; and all other believers around the world, that their yearning for personal and worldwide redemption may soon be satisfied through the working of your grace. Bless the memories and hopes that are brought before this altar and sanctify the songs and prayers we offer, that they may worthily magnify your name and give glory to him who was born in a stable and laid in a manger. Amen.

57

A Pastoral Prayer for the Sunday After Christmas

We have run our yearly race to Bethlehem, O God, and many of us are tired from lives that have been busy and cluttered. Did you mean it to be that way? Surely you intended for your Son's birth to bring us peace and joy and renewal, and a sense of collectedness and togetherness, of being in touch with life's deepest mysteries and realities. Grant that, sorting through the debris of Christmas, we may find that sense of being in touch, and may breathe easier, knowing that you are at work in the world, continuing to become incarnate in the acts of love and fellowship begun in your Son, Jesus. As we near the end of another year, we pray for the overtures of peace that were made this year, that they may find root in honest desire and grow in an atmosphere of trust and goodwill. We remember the poor, and ask that we may find ways to feed them; and the sick, that they may receive healing. We pray for the grieving, that their hearts may be comforted; for the lonely, that they may find relationship; for the fearful, that they may be given confidence; for the doubtful, that they may have faith; for the cynical, that they may experience trust; and for all children and young people, that they may be kept from harmful ways until they are wise enough to withstand temptation. Grant to your church courage and strength and endurance. Help us to covet your leadership above riches and power and earthly approval. Teach us to find you in quietness and follow you in faithfulness, and we shall praise you with the angels and archangels forever and ever. Amen.

58

A Pastoral Prayer for New Year Sunday

O God, who is around every corner we turn, ready to receive us and help us with our new beginnings, we come to you at the start of a new year and kneel before your holiness and power. Erase the bad starts we have made in life: the poor decisions, the wrong commitments, the failures of intuition and courage, the mistakes of heart. Teach us how to listen to you and to submit our wills to yours. Let the righteousness that was in Christ be in us as well. Show us where to turn with what we have left of our lives, and how to invest them for the greatest good. Enable us to love, to reach out to others, to share what we have with the world. We do not want to be selfish or greedy or short-sighted; we want to belong to you and your kingdom; we want our lives to count for something in eternity. Let this be the year in which we learn to pray and to discern your leadership in our affairs, in which we learn to relax and know you are in charge of the world, in which we feel strong and good within ourselves because we know we are striving to do your will. Let it be a year of growth and productivity in the world, when more poor people are fed, when more Third World countries become self-sufficient, when more illiterate men and women learn to read, when more abused children find love and security, when more people who dwell in darkness accept the illumination that was in Christ. If it is within your will, let it be the year when beneficent new treaties are signed, when stockpiles of arms are destroyed, when cures are found for cancer and AIDS and other terminal, crippling diseases, when much new housing is built for the poor, and when the economies of the world are designed less for the rich and more for the masses. Help us to feel your presence here so mightily today that it will enable us to go away resolving to take some important step in our own lives, that tomorrow will be better than today, and the day after that even better than tomorrow. For you are the God of everything new and good and wonderful, and your name shall be praised forever and ever, through Jesus Christ our Lord. Amen.

59

A Pastoral Prayer for New Year Sunday

In the stillness, O God, our hearts turn to you as the needle of a compass points to true North. Amidst all the tension of our world and the turmoil of our lives, you remain at the center, calling us to hope and clarity of purpose. Forgive, we pray, the sins that have confused us and caused us to miss the right direction. Lead us back into the way by your Holy Spirit. On the eve of a new year, give guidance to the nations of the world. Incline our hearts to modesty, honesty, and compassion. Let us be tender to all of those in need, especially the young, the old, the tired, and the poor. Hear our prayers for the sick, whose bodies require rest and mending. Uphold those who grieve, whose spirits are vexed by the loss of loved ones or of position or place held near and dear. Speak to us in our worship, we pray, in something heard or seen or felt, that we may go from this act of praising you with a renewed sense of your presence in our lives and become givers to the world instead of takers. In the name of Christ Jesus our Lord. Amen.

60

O God, whose love is like a gentle, warm wind in a cold and barren country, in this moment we open ourselves to you as we really are. We are children whose values are often confused, so that we strive and spend for that which will not last. We are sheep who wander away from the shepherd, tempted by a few tufts of grass that lie beyond the path. As we look back across the year, we are reminded of two things. First, we remember your faithfulness, and then we remember our waywardness. Forgive us, O warm and gentle One, and lead us back into the way that we should walk. Teach us to wait daily upon you, that your desires may be established in our lives. Grant to our leaders commitment to honesty and peace and justice. Develop in us a care for the poor and hungry and neglected of the world. Shape us as a church into wise and compassionate followers of Jesus. Heal our sick. Give hope to the depressed and grace to the disappointed. Inspire us with your presence, and let us enter a new year with the confidence of those whose Lord is timeless and whose salvation is everlasting. For yours are the hours and the days and the centuries. Amen.

61
A Pastoral Prayer for a Time of Winter Storms

Once more, O God, we have seen the enormous power and majesty of your creation. As roads and pathways became clogged with snow and traffic and commerce came to a halt, we remembered how finite and insignificant we really are. We had a chance to sit in our homes and reflect on our scale of values. Some of us got in touch with our inner lives again and vowed to stay in touch. Some became reacquainted with members of our families and learned how rich our human environment really is. Some of us discovered our neighbors and how capable of kindness and concern they are. Some studied old photograph albums and gave thanks for the richness of our past lives. Some read books or watched TV programs that made us realize how soaring the human spirit can be when it is free and loving. Some of us tasted food again—truly tasted it—and gave thanks for it. What we learned, O God, is the glory of life when it is lived at a decent pace, when we take time to be thoughtful, when we put our arms around one another and experience love, when we bow our heads and express our gratitude to you. We pray for our brothers and sisters for whom the weather has been a great hardship. But we thank you for what the storm has taught us again, and we ask that we may not soon forget its lessons. For yours is the glory of the creation, and we are your creation too, through Jesus Christ. Amen.

62

God of the snow and ice, and God of the thawing fields, we bow before you now in the changing of the seasons and confess to changing seasons in our own lives. We may appear stable to others, but we know the fluctuations that are always taking place in our inner selves. First we doubt and then we have faith. We care about something and then we lose interest. We are strong and then we are weak. We are determined and then lackadaisical. Sometimes it is all we can do to bear our own inconstancy. But you, O God, are always the same with us: strong, gentle, long-suffering, forbearing in love. Teach us to wait on you and be like you, to find in your nature what we lack in our own, and, finding it, to become imitators of you. Let us be followers of our Lord Jesus, whose vision of your kingdom kept him always on course and always devoted to the welfare of others. Help us to care less about ourselves and our reputations and what we have in the world, and more about the poor and the hungry and the lonely people around us. Anoint our sick and wounded with your healing power and grant rest to the weary and overborne. Illuminate a path in the wilderness for our children, and a way in the desert for all of us. And visit us always, in our changing seasons, with a sense of your steadfastness, O God, our rock and our salvation, that we may praise you through Christ Jesus our Lord. Amen.

63

A Pastoral Prayer for Palm Sunday

O Lord of earthquake, fire, and storm, yet Lord of the still, small voice that speaks within the human heart, teach us how to listen to you each day of our lives: how to hear your whispers of love and mercy, inviting us to find fullness of life by seeking your face; how to read the signs of your direction for living in the world, not with grasping or holding, but with celebration and sharing; how to respond to your shouts of disapproval that many of your children are being left to starve or sleep in the cold or work in an unhealthy environment. It is so easy for us to live thoughtlessly and selfishly and even to line the roads for Jesus, the way those people did on the first Palm Sunday, without understanding what it means to be committed to him and the truth for which he died. We rise, eat, work, eat again, and at the end of the day we sleep, all in an endless succession of days. And if we do not think of you, or listen to you, or praise your name, how much better are we than the animals in the field or the thoughtless persons who live as the animals do? Show us a better way, O Lord, and draw us into it. Let our days become testaments of consciousness and love, linking with one another as parts of a journey of growth and devotion, bringing us at last to the foot of your heavenly throne, where we shall fall down in worship and adoration, filled with a sense of your worth and glory forever. Grant strength and peace, we pray, to all your children who suffer from illness or loss this day, and be merciful to all who pass through times of difficulty and confusion. Enable the strong to bear the burdens of the weak and the loving to absorb the unhappiness of those who have been ill-treated. Grant peace and joy to our visitors and let them feel the welcome of this altar. Help us to walk with Christ through this holy, somber week, remembering his suffering, savoring his love, and preparing our hearts for the Day of Resurrection, when we shall sing and dance and praise your name forever! Amen.

64
A Pastoral Prayer for Palm Sunday

O God, who knows all about palm branches and crowds of well-wishers and then betrayal and loneliness, we confess to you that we have not always been loyal to you or to the highest insights you have given us, and, if we are sad this morning, it is because we have not matured fully into the people of love and grace and joy we would have liked to become. Help us to make of this hour a turning point in our lives. If we have come here in confusion, give us clarity and direction before we leave. If we have come in anger, give us peace and the resolution of our feelings. If we have come with doubts, lead us to faith. If we have come in apathy, ignite our passion. If we have come in loneliness, show us how to have fellowship. If we have come in weakness, fill us with your power. Reveal yourself so strongly to our minds and hearts that we may be transformed into true, stouthearted followers of the Savior. Let your grace fall especially on our visitors, that their lives in the coming week may be fulfilled and happy. Watch over our children in this age of drugs and crime, and help us to give them safe and instructive passage until they reach an age of personal accountability. We lift up to you our president and other officers of the government, that they may be given the wisdom and stamina to cope with the problems of a world that often seems to be out of control. Let your Spirit be upon this church, that it may fulfill its mission of love and redemption in the world, caring for the poor and disenfranchised, providing fellowship for all within its walls, and offering the gospel to hungry, wayward souls. Amid all the hurry and worry of our days and in the shallow culture of our times, let your kingdom come, O Lord our God and our eternal hope. Amen.

65

A Pastoral Prayer for Holy Week

O Lord of Holy Week, as you are Lord of all time; O Lord of Jerusalem, as you are Lord of all cities; O Lord of the Apostles, as you are Lord of all followers; we bow before you in humble contrition for all our sin: for our failure to become what we might have been; for our inability to see what we ought to see; for our incapacity to love as we would like to love. Receive us in our brokenness as you received Simon Peter, and set us once more on the high road to purity and service. Let our hearts and minds be formed around our meeting with you, that there may be wholeness and goodness in all our acts and being. Teach us to esteem others better than ourselves and to care more for their welfare than our own. Show us how to use what you have entrusted to us for the redemption of our community and our world. Give strength to those whose way is difficult and light to those whose way is dark. Enable us to reach out to one another in times of grief or illness and to embrace one another across lines of difference. Guide the leaders of the nations, that they may be wise in the pursuit of peace, and guide all their peoples, that we may support them through prayer and devotion to you. Now draw us together in heart and purpose as we continue to worship you, and let the spirit of the cross and resurrection be upon us in power and grace, for this hour and evermore. Amen.

66

A Pastoral Prayer for Easter

In the midst of life, O God, we are surrounded by death: the death of hope, the death of desire, the death of ambition, the death of innocence, the death of programs, the death of institutions, the death of promises, the death of those we love, the death that works in our own bodies. Therefore we give you thanks for the gospel of Jesus Christ, whose message is not death but life: the life of the Spirit, the life of dreams, the life of faith, the life of love, the life of justice, life for the small people of the world, life for the meek, life for the broken and rejected, life for the diseased and afflicted, life for our dear ones, life for us. Help us to turn our backs on death as negation and to discover it as affirmation: dying into Christ, dying to self, dying to false ambitions, dying to pride, dying to loneliness and sin, living for Christ, living for those around us, living for the world, living for the environment, living for the kingdom, living to the utmost. Teach us to live every moment of our lives. Let the Christ of the empty tomb make empty tombs of all our defeats. Come and reign over us, Ancient of Days, now and evermore. Amen.

67

A Pastoral Prayer for Easter

O God of the cross and the empty tomb, whose power is known in our lives today through the coming of Spring, the witness of the church, and the urgency we feel to worship you, we bow our heads before you in humility and contrition and awe. You are the God who created the world. You are the God who produced a reluctant servant-nation in Israel. You are the God who sent our Lord Jesus to be offered as a sacrifice and then raised from death. You are the God who brought forth the church and aided it in its long struggle against evil and confusion and corruption. You are the God who has declared your love for the poor, the broken, the diseased, and the hungry of the world. You are the God of our loved ones who have preceded us in death and are even now gathered about your throne in eternity. And you are the God who has called us, the people within this sanctuary, to be your servants and stewards and witnesses. You have entrusted to each of us a portion of your mystery and beauty and holiness, and you have said: "Share these with your family and your friends and all the world around you." We ask your forgiveness, O God, for the many ways we have failed you: by being selfish, by seeking our own pleasures in life, by ignoring your commandments and your call upon us. Restore us now to your service, we pray. Let a sense of your Holy Spirit—of being caught up in a new attitude toward ourselves and our place in the world—come upon us, reshaping us, retooling us, redirecting us into the way of worship and obedience. Let the glories of this Easter morning, with its bursting flowers and blooming trees and springing grass, be as nothing beside the joy and peace released into our hearts as we recommit ourselves to you in love and excitement. And grant that we may go from here as your Easter people, as sons and daughters of the Resurrection, to restore health and wholeness and order to a world you love so deeply, through Jesus Christ our Lord. Amen.

68
A Pastoral Prayer for Easter

We remember many things on this special morning, O Lord: the thrill of a new bonnet or a new pair of shoes; the colored eggs hidden in the grass; the scent of lilies in the air; the great music; the crowds of people in church, on the streets, in the restaurants; the feeling of newness in the world; the sense of something transcendent, reaching beyond this world and uniting it with the life beyond. We praise you for the transcendence, for the awareness of divine presence, for the knowledge that when all earth's stories are told, of war and famine and disease and suffering, there is something else, another story, of a Man who truly lived and loved and gave himself, who died on a cross and was raised to new life out of the very grave itself. How different our lives are because of this story, Lord. How different the world is because of it! We hold before you today the entire community of faith in every part of the world—brothers and sisters in Christ in Zimbabwe, Brazil, Korea, Nicaragua, Pakistan, and wherever hands are lifted to you in prayer. Let us all remember the victory of Christ and live in the coming triumph of your kingdom. Even where there is fighting and sickness and starvation, where people die and there is much sadness, grant that there may be also a mood of hope and expectancy, an inner certainty that you will not forsake those to whom you have revealed and promised so much in your Son Jesus. We know that night is often darkest before the dawn, and therefore we are bold to pray even now, when there is so much unrest and injustice in the world, that your redemption may quickly come; that little children may grow up in a world without drugs; that mothers and fathers may always love one another; that the elderly may walk on the streets without fear; that the poor will be fed from the tables of the rich, and the homeless sheltered in the houses of the wealthy; and that all people will resort daily to the altars and sanctuaries of the Most High, to give you thanks and to receive your blessing and to live peaceably and joyfully with all their neighbors. To that end, receive and bless our worship here this day and let your name be praised in glory by all the saints and angels, both here and in eternity, forever and ever. Amen.

69
A Pastoral Prayer for Easter

The Gospels do not tell us, O God, what kind of day it was when Jesus rose from the grave. Perhaps it was a day like this—cold and wet and dark. Yet it turned the inner landscapes of the disciples into soulscapes of eternal spring and sunshine, and brightened their lives with the glory of a presence that changed the very way they looked at the world. Grant that we may have that experience today. Let the risen Christ commune with us as he did with his followers then, and transform us from straggling, unworthy churchgoers into men and women and boys and girls of stalwart faith, ready to undertake any task or defy any danger to serve you in the world beyond these walls. Forgive us for thinking death and grave and dreariness when you are thinking resurrection and life and excitement. Help us to feel the power of faith—to let it surge through our hearts and bodies—and then let it flow through us to the poor and sick and confused and disheartened of the world. Show us how to feed the hungry, shelter the homeless, educate the illiterate, embrace the outcast, claim the wayward, and love the enemy. Make this the day when your gospel is truly heard in our lives—though we thought we had heard it a hundred times before—and we become your enthusiastic, obedient servants. Through Jesus Christ our Lord. Amen.

70

O God, whose presence is like a fountain of fresh water springing up in a desert place, we come today to drink from you. Our lives are parched and dry from traveling through arid places. Our souls are desiccated from the pressures and hardships of existence. Receive us now with openness and quench our thirst. Let the weak find strength and courage. Give pardon to the wayward and friendship to the lonely. Heal the sick and bind up the brokenhearted. Provide respite for the exhausted and clarity for the confused. Teach us to exalt Christ in our living and in our dying. Give wisdom and stamina to our president and other leaders. Grant that our nation, instead of being first in crime, first in drugs, and first in murders, may become first in daring, first in caring, and first in sharing. Anoint your church with new power to proclaim the gospel and prophesy to the world. Help us to set our own house in order, being Christlike in thought and deed, and then to become a channel of grace to all the peoples of the globe. Amplify the voices of those who are kind and gentle, and silence the voices of those who are contentious. Let your peace overtake us in our hurry and worry, and so convert us that we find the world a paradise. Bless the efforts of all charitable agencies, that they may thrive for the good work they try to do. Let love break out like an epidemic, claiming the hearts and minds of millions of people, and let the kingdoms of this world become the kingdom of our Christ, today and forever. Amen.

71

O God, who has given us this good day and enriched it with the sense of your presence here, we thank you for every gift that has enhanced our lives: for the places where we have lived, which fill us with wonderful memories; for places of work and relaxation; for joy in love and peace in relationships; for strength and dexterity and maturity and wisdom; for little children who renew our families and communities; for teachers and singers and artists and engineers; for doctors and lawyers and accountants and homemakers; for smiling faces and the warm touch of hands; for music and games and the sun and the rain. Bless the visitors who are worshiping among us today and grant them, with us, renewal of spirit and joy in everything you have made. Abide with our ill and ailing members and with all who suffer or experience deprivation of any kind. Feed us on your Word and on this wonderful fellowship. Then send us forth as your vibrant missionaries, converted and converting and being converted, until all the world shall become the kingdom of our Lord and we shall worship you forever, O desire of our hearts and lover of our souls. Amen.

72

In the beauty of this place, O God, amid the music and prayers and light filtered through colored glass, we are greatly aware of your presence: of the breath of your Spirit moving around us; of the touch of your hand laid upon us; of the throbbing of your heart beating with ours, establishing a rhythm that will help us to be calm and composed for the lives we shall live. We regret that we are not more persistent and purposeful in our attempts to experience this presence every day of our lives, that we sometimes let hours and days pass without reflecting on your grace and beneficence toward us. Being reminded, we thank you for the most basic gifts of our lives: for bodies and minds that interact, for hearts to love and dream and embrace our enemies, for awareness of the beautiful world around us, for sensitivity to art and music and history, for the animals that enrich our lives, for friends who accept us as we are, for parents who birthed us and children who needed us and spouses whose acceptance and caring have nurtured and shaped us through the years. We lift our prayers for all who suffer illness or anxiety of any kind; for those who endure hardship and privation; for those who struggle with addiction and those with difficult home or work situations; for those with hard decisions to make; for those who act in the positions of servants to make life better for others; for the leaders of our country and of this state; for the poor and homeless and distraught of all the world; and finally for ourselves, that we may be given the will and strength to fulfill our highest aspirations and dreams, provided they will honor you and bless others around us. Through Jesus Christ, our servant Lord. Amen.

73
A Pastoral Prayer for Graduation Sunday

Look upon us in mercy, O God, and let our hearts open before you like flowers in the sunshine. Teach us to live expectantly in your presence, so that we recognize our blessings and respond in cheerful gratitude. Grant that we may shed our anxieties before you like worn and tattered garments and step away from them in joy and newness of life. Lift up the hearts of all who have come here today in depression or despondency. Touch with healing the sick and grieving of our community. Reveal new pathways to those who have become lost or confused in the thickets of life. Show us how to live openly and generously with all your gifts and to grow in wisdom and humanity by sharing them with everyone around us. Lift us out of complacency and give us new and meaningful tasks to do. We are very much aware of the great unrest in our world, and raise our prayers for freedom and justice and peace. Use this congregation and its rich heritage to bless and enrich the city and the world that lie at its doorstep. We celebrate today the lives of all our students, their teachers and administrators, and especially our graduates and their families. Give them the gift of laughter and happiness. Let their memories and joys and commitment rise up like incense in the heart, filling these days with a rich and exquisite perfume of the spirit. As they consider the sadness of knowing that something has come to an end, infuse them with the excitement of what is also being born. Walk with them wherever they go. Teach them to live reverently and joyfully, respecting the needs of others and sharing with them the wealth of their background and abilities. Comfort the mothers and fathers who contemplate with sorrow the swiftness with which change will come to their households. Let them rejoice in the cycle of life and growth that carries children away from home and bestows upon them the blessings of discovery and achievement. Enable us all to pause with a sense of humility before the ever-moving river of time and to remember that you alone do not change but are always the God of our Lord Jesus Christ and the Father of mercy, in whom we live and move and have our being, now and forever. Amen.

74

There is no beauty or worth in us, O God, that you should become our lover and protector, and yet you have. When we were formed in our mothers' wombs, you cared for us. When we struggled as children to understand the world in which we lived, you came at night to kiss our furrowed brows. And now, when we deal with the great complexities and difficulties of adult existence, you are always here to share our burdens and make our suffering bearable. How can we fail to love you and be grateful? And how can we fail to extend a similar care to others who share our lives and our planet: to the poor, whose suffering we can help to alleviate; to the sick, whose welfare we offer up to you in earnest prayer; to the hurt and the lonely, who will feel better with our arms around them; to the discouraged and the jobless, whom we can encourage; to the confused and dispirited, whom we commit to you for special care; and to the dying, along whose way we gather to bid them courage and farewell. Help us to rearrange our own existences, O God, to make more room for you, and for true joy, and for prayer and holiness, and for loving all who touch upon our lives, however briefly; for it is your nature to love and care, and our beings are made whole as we learn to imitate your ways. Through Jesus Christ our Lord. Amen.

75

In a setting like this, O God, we are reminded of your presence and of the fact that we often live from day to day with little awareness of your being there: that we go about our busy ways, conducting our trades and eating our meals and traveling the highways and reading the papers and brushing our teeth, without sensing that you are nearer to us than the things we touch or the people we meet. If we may be granted one prayer, let it be that we may live more sensitively, with eyes to see and ears to hear, with souls to know that you are here, and that your being here makes all the difference in who we are and how we exist. Teach us to live in love and hope, so that we are not always anxious about things that do not matter, and so that we may share with one another the best that we are and not the poorest, as we often do. Let the spirit that was in Christ Jesus our Lord be in us also, guiding and directing our paths toward the fulfillment and happiness you want to give us. We hold before you all our visitors and the concerns of their hearts, and all of our own members who have special needs. Reveal to us ways of sharing who we are and what we possess with others who long for relationship and have need of food or home or medicine or anything else. Consecrate our imaginations to your service, that they may help fulfill our prayer for your kingdom to blossom among us. And now give us delight in the music we hear, the flowers on the altar, the light coming through these windows, the sense of one another's presence, as we wait before you, O God of all the ages and nurturing spirit of our souls. Enfold us in your arms and leave us, when this hour is done, with a sense of eternity. Through Jesus Christ. Amen.

76

Your messages come to us in a thousand ways, O God: in the song of a bird, the sound of the sea, the look of a flag billowing in the breeze, the feeling of raindrops on a hot and muggy day, the taste of a melon, the scent of a flower, the touch of a friend's hand, the look in a child's face, the silence of a midnight, the smell of morning coffee. Forgive us for living a week or a day or even an hour without noticing and praising you, without our hearts crying out, "Oh God, it is so beautiful, and you are so awesome!" Teach us to live sensitively, experiencing joy, bestowing forgiveness, sharing bread, and giving love. Let the sense of your presence that was in Christ Jesus inhabit us as well, that we may walk through our days as living sacraments, embodying faith and spreading light and hope in the world. Bless all our visitors today, give health and strength to those who are ill or troubled, and let those who are lost find their way again. Let all who are discouraged take heart once more, and all who fear their mortality remember the promises of Christ about a life to come that is filled with the joy of saints and angels. For we ask all of this in his name and in the assurance of your continued love and goodwill. Amen.

77

O God, whose mercies are from everlasting and whose tender love goes far beyond any we have ever known, we confess to you our proneness to forget your care and to abuse ourselves with fears and anxieties and self-recriminations. The wonder of our faith is that we are already forgiven for our shortcomings and that all of life stretches before us as a journey of love, discovery, and rejoicing. Grant that something in this service—a song, a word, the flowers on the table, the touch of a neighbor's hand—will remind us of this, and that, feeling a sudden rush in the heart or brain, we may experience our redemption as something real and palpable, something to transform our very existence. Let the cloak of your blessing fall upon our visitors, that they may go their way enriched and enlarged. Hear our prayers for all whose health is threatened or precarious and for those whose way is made difficult by other problems or extremities. Send your consolation upon those who have lost loved ones and still find their days dark and heavy with grief. Let the victory at the heart of the first Christian experience become the victory in our hearts at all times, and help us to share this until the entire world is filled with the wonder of your name. Through Christ our risen Lord. Amen.

78

There is a presence here, O God, that deepens and strengthens our lives. It is a mystery we do not need to understand. We have only to feel it to know that it is real. It is like a fountain in dry land, like sunshine after days and days of cloudiness, like the arms of a friend after a long, long journey. Teach us to seek it daily, O God, and not to wait for special occasions. Help us to be conscious of you at our work, in our play, when we shop, when we eat, wherever we are. Let the joy and serenity of our lives then become a witness to others who need you in their lives, and thus enable your kingdom to come in the world. We remember today our friends who are ill at home or in the hospital and ask for their recovery. We pray for those who have lost friends or family members to death, that they may find comfort. We lift up those who have lost jobs or had difficulties in school or experienced broken relationships with others; minister to their hurt and embarrassment, and let them find new purpose and direction in life. Guard those who travel. Give blessing to loved ones who are far away from us. Protect and inspire our young people. Strengthen and direct our president and other officers of the government. Send peace and love into the hearts of all people. Show us how to live gracefully in the earth without damaging our environment. Guide especially the destinies of developing nations. Grant us a spirit of sensitivity and caring, that we may be good stewards of all our gifts. Let this church be a home to the wounded who seek shelter here and a beacon of light to this community in a time of change and alteration. May Christ be glorified in all we say or think or do, and may we find rest and peace beneath his cross. Send your Spirit upon us and bind us together in love and goodwill, and teach us to rejoice in that which passes all human understanding. For your name's sake. Amen.

79

O God, whose love is as refreshing as a summer rain, yet searching as the summer sun, we open our hearts to you now in quietness and humility, asking for your Holy Spirit to come among us. We know we have not served you as we should. Most of our thoughts and efforts have been for ourselves. We have not remembered the beggar at our gates, or the loved one crying for attention, or the young man sitting in the county jail, or the poor woman dying of disease and malnutrition in the slums. What can we say to you, O God, except that we are guilty—guilty of not seeing, guilty of not caring, guilty of not loving. Forgive us, dear God. We have taken the name of Christ without his mission, without his cross, without his concern. Teach us the things that really matter in life. Help us not to spend our energies on trifles or worry about what doesn't matter. Help us to see both large issues and specific needs. Use us as your servants in the world to fight evil and injustice wherever they exist. Lift up the hearts of those who are ill, that they may know the center of all healing. Grant the spirit of true forgiveness and joy to all who have lived under the tyranny of guilt and self-doubt. Give life and viability to this community of faith, that it may turn to your kingdom's use all who come to it; and show us the way to love and fellowship, through Christ and your Holy Spirit. Amen.

80

Gracious God, whose presence is felt in the beauty of the world and in the hush of this sanctuary, how easy it is for us to forget the areas of the globe where people are suffering: places where there is hunger and disease and fighting and imprisonment and death without dignity; hospitals and old age homes and abortion clinics and penitentiaries and orphanages and detention houses and ghettos and places of hard labor. Most of the time we are so insulated from the degradation and horrors of life suffered by many of your children that we don't even remember to pray for them or to be grateful for our own conditions. Forgive us, O God, for ever complaining about our situations. Remind us that we are one with all who need or suffer. Teach us to care for them and to take steps to help them. Let every child be ambitious to make the world a better place and every adult eager to reach out with food and money and clothing and books and medicine and whatever else will make life more decent and just for all your people in all the world. Make justice a preoccupation of our minds, as it was of Christ's, and a burning desire of our hearts, as it was of his. Grant healing to our friends who are sick and comfort to those who are lonely for loved ones. Draw us close to you in our daily living until we have peace in our souls and joy in all we do. And enable us to praise you now, that our spirits may be caught up in your one great Spirit and we may understand what it is to worship you in spirit and in truth, through Jesus Christ our Savior. Amen.

81

O God, who created the great giraffes that glide through the jungles and the little slugs that slither among the flowers in our gardens, we praise you for the glories of your creation: for children and laughter, for songs and clouds, for mountains and seas, for birds and cats, for storms and sunshine and honeysuckle blossoms. O God, who gives us joy in the morning and rest at night, and teaches us to see the world with wholeness and contentment of spirit, we exalt your name for the love you have shown us: for the patience with our sinning; for the gift of your Son Jesus and his ministry, death, and resurrection; for our new life in the kingdom; for teachers who instruct us and for friends who care; for existence in this world and hope in the next one. We remember today our friends in the hospital and those who are ill or confined at home. Let your healing spirit be upon them to mend their bodies and lift their hearts and give them peace. We pray for the peace of the world wherever there is conflict or oppression. Grant that we may all learn to contribute to the justice, equality, and harmony of our common life around the globe. We bless in your name all teachers, ministers, social workers, and other servants of the common good. Give us spirits eager to learn of your will for our energies and resources, that we may maximize our cooperation and contributions. Instill in our president and other public officials a strong desire to share the benefits of our rich land with the poor and broken and uneducated peoples of the world, that they may lead us into ways of blessing the nations. Now minister, we pray, to the hurts and needs of our own congregation gathered here today. Give courage to the weak and hope to the despondent. Redirect the wills of those who have gone astray and comfort the hearts of the lonely. Enable us so to share together the experience of Christ's presence that we shall feel bonded to one another and to you and thus emerge from this hour stronger and more centered and more committed to life than ever before, in the name of him who died and rose and now reigns with you, eternal in the heavens, world without end. Amen.

82

O God, whose mystery is as deep as the fog that sometimes shrouds our land, yet who has shown yourself clearly in the love and teachings of Jesus, we praise you for the faith that has brought us together and for the great line of saints whose lives and witness have conspired to make believers of us across the years. Forgive, we pray, the busyness and indifference that have often characterized our spirits, so that we have not lived with either the joy or the commitment that might have marked our daily lives. Draw us back into your way that we may experience redemption as sick persons experience recovery, and show us how to redesign our existence in keeping with your eternal plan. We remember the desperateness of the world beyond our walls, and bow in prayer for the many peoples of our globe. Some have inadequate food and water and medical care, and many languish in ignorance and superstition. Teach us to share our own resources with them in such a way that the world may no longer be divided between those who have and those who don't. Give healing to those of our number who are ill or anxious today and remind us of the power of your Spirit to transform every earthly situation. Gift us with a word that will challenge our self-satisfaction and raise our eyes to new horizons of love and self-giving, that we may glorify you in all we think and say and do. For you are God and we are your humble people, through Jesus Christ our Lord. Amen.

83

O God, whose mercy often comes as a fire that burns, chastening and purifying existence, we thank you for your everlasting love made known in Christ, who died for our sins, and in your Holy Spirit, who warms our hearts when we are together in you. There is much in our lives that keeps us from enjoying peace and wholeness in the world: a lack of discipline, a rush to judgment, an impetuousness of speech, a basic selfishness, anxieties of the heart and mind, an inability to believe in ourselves or in other persons or in you. Forgive our weaknesses and failures, O God, and increase our faith. Let us become so related to you through Christ, so drawn to your mystery and love, that our earthly natures give way to heavenly natures and we learn to live in paradise right where we are, under the world's conditions of adversity and struggle and defeat. Teach us to bear suffering with Christ in order that we may know the fulfillment and joy of the resurrection. Let this church become a center of your Spirit's activities in this community and in the world beyond. Show us how to use everything we are and have and hope to be for the sake of your eternal kingdom, thus defying time and change and hardship and injustice. Grant tender mercies to all who have endured the loss of loved ones in recent weeks and months. Walk with those who have had bad news and give them patience and courage and hope. Continue to strengthen those who undergo a long struggle of the human spirit. Send love and growth upon all couples recently married or about to be married and on all children who live in homes of divorce or unhappiness. And let your Spirit so rule in our lives that we may gladly deny ourselves and take up our crosses and follow Christ, this day and forever. Amen.

84

As the earth longs for gentle drops of rain, O God, our souls thirst for the coming of your Spirit. We are dry and arid without you, and our lives are barren and unproductive. Teach us to compose ourselves to receive you: to see you at work in the world and the people around us; to be quiet and listen for your still, small voice; to be submitted and ready to do your will when we know it. Give us obedient hearts, O God, to perform the things you have already required of us: to love one another, to care for the poor and hungry, to live as touching eternity, and to act justly and truthfully in all our endeavors. Let your healing hand rest softly today on all who are passing through times of illness or grief. Grant assurance and confidence to those who are doubting or afraid. Inspire our children with visions of discipleship and save them from the more demonic aspects of our culture. Bless all teachers with a sense of your presence. Give heart to your ministers. Let your Word be experienced as a flashing sword, cutting to the marrow of all the issues faced in our time. And in your mercy let it be that the person who sits here now in silence and aimlessness, with little sense of what this is all about, may suddenly feel the updrafts and downdrafts of your Holy Spirit and, knowing that he or she is in the presence of a mystery beyond all human thought or understanding, will fall down before you in wonder and worship. Through Jesus Christ, who lives and walks among us forever and ever. Amen.

85

You have given us eyes, O God, but we see so little; ears, but we hear so little; hearts, but we love so little. The world around us is a treasure-trove of gifts: dancing leaves and the smell of smoke; geese on the wing and children playing; fields of grain and kitchen larders; cars and boats and buildings and houses; fast-food chains and TVs and shopping centers; friends and families and a nation of plenty. Why are we so often unhappy and discontented? Is it you, O God? Have we reveled in gifts and missed the giver?

Have we accepted the evidences of your love and forgotten the love itself? Forgive us, dear God, and turn us again to wholeness and perception. Let the mind that was in Christ Jesus be in us as well, to walk humbly in the world and to see everything with the eyes of children, who rejoice in dandelions and colored leaves, who skip rope and ponder the clouds, who dwell in the day they have without trying to save everything for tomorrow. And let us live with true thanksgiving in our hearts, remembering your love and presence, which would turn even the desert into a paradise and which are freely ours in him who said, "Do you have eyes, and fail to see? Do you have ears, and fail to hear?"* Amen.

86

O God, whose glory is above that of the angels, yet who has entered our lives in the man Jesus and walked the dusty roads of care and toil beside us, we bow before you in humble awareness of our sinful conditions. Your goodness is so far beyond ours, and your power so much greater than any we have known, that we are unworthy even to speak your name. Yet you have forgiven us and claimed us and taught us to call you Father. What can we say before such mercy and love? Turn us around, Father. Show us new ways to live; give us new courage to face our trials; reveal to us new images for considering who we are. Let us live as the sons and daughters of the Most High, with joy and peace filling our souls. Help us to be merciful toward those to whom we can show mercy: on the poor, whom our generosity can help; on little children, who look to us for guidance; on the lonely, who would cherish our visits and cards and letters; on the doubtful, who would be enriched by our faith and witness; on the struggling, whose way would be made easier by our love and encouragement. Relieve us of our preoccupation with self and what belongs to us, that we may

---

* Mark 8:18.

rejoice in the knowledge that everything belongs to you, including ourselves. Let us worship you even in grief or in illness by exclaiming, "The earth is the LORD's and all that is in it."* Visit us in our frailty and help us to be people of strength. Come to us in our apathy and neglect and show us how to be people of caring. Descend to us in our sickness and brokenness and make us people of wholeness and love. For you are the God of all goodness and power, you are the Father of mercies. Through Jesus Christ our Lord. Amen.

87

O God, we thank you for the world of our senses: for sight and sound and taste and touch and smell, for puppies and kittens and cactus flowers and avocados; for sunsets and rainbows and billowing clouds and gently falling rain; for oatmeal and bananas and lobsters and peanut butter; for perfumes and paintings and pollywogs and pomegranates; for friends and families and new grapes and old wine; for youth and age and the years in between; for books and banners and symphonies and serendipity; for all the thousands of items and experiences that constitute our lives and our environment and our time in history. We thank you for the world of our history and the growth of our understanding through the years: for church and reformers; for mystics and pilgrims; for printing and reading and schools and languages; for knowledge of the mind and disciplines of the body; for sciences of the earth and sciences of space; for banking and trade and courts and clubs; for the whole network of human caring and protectionism that safeguards our liberties, ensures our health, and provides for our wellbeing as groups and individuals. But most of all, O God, we thank you for the Word you have spoken in Christ, that gives meaning and order to everything else, so that we are not

---

* Psalm 24:1.

mere aesthetes and humanists and epicureans, but pilgrims bound for a fuller existence in the world to come, where all our senses shall be quickened and multiplied into a total apprehension of eternal life itself, and you will be all in all, the center and completeness of everything, ground of all being, glorious destination of all that has ever been, is now, or ever shall be. To that end, do receive our worship and adoration in this hour, heal us of all fragmentedness and failure, and make us your joyous allies in the process of reconciling the world to yourself. Through Jesus Christ our Lord. Amen.

88

O Lord, teach us how to pray as you taught your disciples of old. Help us to begin by meditating on you and your presence until our hearts swell up in praise for you and we desire your kingdom more than anything else in the world. Then let us ask you simply for the few things in life we need: our daily bread and drink, a little sunshine, the love of a friend or two, and your forgiveness, which makes our humanity acceptable in the face of your great holiness and in turn enables us to be accepting of others. Remind us to pray for true commitment, that we will not be thoughtlessly swept away from our faith by the many small commitments of our lives and wake up one day to find ourselves the prisoners of darkness and evil. And finally, let us pause before we are through to remember again your kingdom, and to realize that you have the power to make it a reality for us in this world now, and may the realization elicit from each of us a spontaneous sigh of praise that will add its little weight to your great glory for the day. For yours *are* the kingdom and the power and the glory, not only today but always. Amen.

89

O God, whose love is from everlasting and whose way is filled with peace, our world is in urgent need today. Our greed has overtaken the ability of our environment to heal itself. Our reluctance to share has resulted in great imbalance among the nations. Our politics have led us into bitterness and resentment. Even our religion has betrayed us into pride and prejudice and division. Bring us back to yourself, O God, and into the way of loving fellowship. Let friendship triumph over hostility and caring over selfishness. Make families whole and gentle again and communities accepting and restorative. Teach us the old virtues of faithfulness, service, duty, honor, integrity, and character, and make us willing once more to sacrifice our own gain for the public good. Lead us in paths of righteousness for your name's sake, and by the still waters of quiet devotion, that we may be inwardly renewed by your own divine life and spirit. Bestow joy and contentment on the friends who visit us today and watch over with tender care our friends who are away. Attend to our loved ones in all parts of the globe with healing and happiness, and continue to lead us in the spirit of your Son Jesus, who endured death on a cross for the heavenly joy that was set before him. Amen.

90

You are here, O God, even when we are unaware of it, touching our lives with grace in a thousand ways: in the smiles of people we pass, the gurgling sounds of babies, the flowers growing where we didn't expect them, the taste of warm bread, the sight of a hawk sailing in a clear blue sky, the rustle of leaves, a letter from someone we love, the warmth of a friend's voice, the security of a favorite room in the house, the view from a window, the comfort of an old pair of shoes. How wonderfully rich our lives are, and how seldom we praise you. Teach us to see with new eyes the wonders that surround us. Make us into children again, for whom the world is vibrant with color and texture and magic. Take away our tiredness, our habit of not being present, our dullness to all that is beautiful and holy. Make us sensitive to one another and to where you are moving in our lives. Bless the visitors who worship with us and hear the supplications of their hearts. Heal our sick. Give rest to the weary. Comfort the grieving. Inspire our leaders. And show us how to celebrate the resurrection every day of our lives. Through Christ our Lord. Amen.

91

Our Father, Jesus suggested, somewhat audaciously, that you are like a woman who had a number of coins but, when she lost one, could not rest until she had turned her house upside down to find it. This means that you care about our loved ones who die and about us who remain behind. It means that you care about the elderly who have said good-bye to their youth and strength and stamina and to their former positions and even their former families. It means that you care about all who have lost their jobs or failed in their undertakings or experienced loneliness and frustration. It means that you care about the street people who come to us for food or lodging. It means that you care about this church and its work in this place. We bow before such care, O Father, and give thanks for your never-failing love. Grant that we, as a congregation, may learn to care and love as you do. Let the faithfulness that carried your Son Jesus to a cross carry us to any extremity as well. Teach us to be so committed to you that our lives will find their natural centers in you and not in the world around us. Grant that our nation, with its great power and prestige, may strive to serve the common good of all peoples and to facilitate the day when the kingdoms of this earth shall become the kingdom of our Christ. Let your hand of healing be upon the sick, the lonely, the bereaved, the lost, the depressed, and the desperate, and grant that we may all be channels of hope and restitution to those around us, both here and in other important places of our lives. Through Christ Jesus our Lord. Amen.

92

A Pastoral Prayer for Young People

In the midst of an ever-changing world, O God, you are always there, steadfast and immutable, like an eternal rock to which we can anchor our small skiffs. We assemble here this morning aware of the way life moves on, an ever-flowing stream, and bears us away from where we began. The world turns, history marches on, and our individual lives are no longer what they were. The child becomes the adult and then the child again. People enter and leave our lives, and we live with impressions of hundreds of folk once unknown to us. We bless the process of living, O God, and turn our consciousness to you, who imparts life and grace and peace to all. We celebrate today the lives of our young people and the changes occurring in their minds and bodies. We thank you for the renewing that will come to this church through them: for their devotion to Christ, for their indomitable spirit in the face of adversity, for the adventure of living that preoccupies them, for the hope and innocence in their faces that helps us to have faith in the future. Grant them a strong sense of your presence during these difficult times. Help them to build their lives on the solid foundation of faith and love. Save them from the temptation to surrender purity of heart for popularity that will not last and goodness of spirit for the thrill that dies the moment it is born. Let those of us who are older prove to be caring and faithful servants of the mysteries of Christ on their behalf, that they may come daily closer to grasping these mysteries themselves. When they do fail, let them not be ashamed to seek help; and when they seek help, let them find it, as we have all found it, in the grace of our Lord Jesus Christ. Now, receive the worship which we offer to you, young and old alike, and let it be pleasant in your sight, O God. Heal us of all that wears and corrupts us, and let us sing praises to your great name now and forever more. Amen.

93

O Lord, who gives us the seasons of the year that the earth may be refreshed and renewed and gives us the seasons of our lives that we may be reborn with new hearts and new purposes for living, we lay before you now our thoughts and hopes and dreams. Stir them with the wind of your Spirit, that they may assume the patterns of your will. Be especially close to those who face important decisions about the future and also to those whose lives are so encumbered that they seem to have no decisions to make. Help us to live each season fully, relying on your love to amplify all our possibilities. We make our prayers today for all the people of the world who are not able to live fully because of unfavorable conditions; for those who live in hunger zones; for those without educational opportunities; for those in prison; for those whose lives are spent in ghettos; and for those who exist under any kind of social, religious, or political repression. May the government of our own country be so attuned to its moral responsibilities, both at home and abroad, that it will shine like a beacon of hope in the darkness of the world's despair. Grant to our church a clear vision of our own obligations to the thousands of people around us who will not hear the gospel unless we preach it, who will not eat unless we feed them, who will have no place to sleep unless we provide beds, who will not learn to read unless we teach them, who will not know that other people care unless we reach out to embrace them. May Christ walk these aisles today, calling to those who ought to follow him, touching those who are ill, encouraging those who are in despair, comforting those who have experienced loss, and sharing himself with those who have felt abandoned or alone. Let your words find lodging in our hearts and let our songs of praise find acceptance in your courts, O Father and Mother of all, O Savior and Redeemer of the world. Amen.

94

We wait in quietness, O God, for your Spirit to fall upon us, changing us into the souls we would like to offer you. Therefore we ask that you will take away our fretfulness and anxiety and give us peace and joy. Remove our proneness to anger and outrage and give us gentleness of spirit. Lift us above our fear and shyness and let us be happy and outgoing. As we drink from the common cup of Christ's sacrifice, teach us to be united in a spirit of love. We remember today the many hurting and disadvantaged people of the world: the poor and homeless, the sick and disabled, the lost and bereaved, the abused and addicted, the jobless and imprisoned, the illiterate and dysfunctional, the old and tired, the bored and disenchanted. Let your kingdom come, Lord, and produce a reordering of human sensibilities and priorities. Bless all who labor to assist such a transformation, and increase the role of this church in bringing it about through prayer and personal involvement. Guide us today as we worship you here, and then as we greet one another in love and fellowship. Let your Spirit especially support and revitalize our visitors, that they may go on their way refreshed by your presence, and grant that we may all stand taller and experience a greater freedom of spirit for having been here. Through Christ, who bids us follow him. Amen.

95

O mighty Healer, who makes well our bodies and our spirits and our world, we feel better for being in your presence. Something happens to us here. Our hearts are cleansed. Our bodies relax. Our sensibilities grow keener. Our sympathies are enlarged. Our vision of the future is expanded. We praise you, O God, for the power that changes things: that takes people with disabilities and makes them whole, that takes twisted minds and makes them straight, that takes a confused and bleeding world and turns it into a paradise. We stand today on the edge of a better tomorrow and ask your help in descrying what shape it should take. Grant peace in the hearts of all who are gathered here today. Give joy especially to our visitors, that something said or done, some smile or touch bestowed by another, may remind them of the mysteries of the Master and release in them the sweet perfume of his presence. Bestow strength on the weak, rest on the weary, light on the perplexed, comfort on the bereaved, faith on the doubtful, hope on the despairing, and companionship on the lonely. And let us all find cause for celebration as we remember the past and look to the future, through Jesus Christ our Savior, the Lord of this world and the next. Amen.

96

O God of sunshine and shadow, God of pain and joy, we lay before you now our mingled stories of success and failure, acceptance and rejection, happiness and sadness. Relate to each of us in the way in which we need you most. Let your Spirit, which has come to people in times of articulated need as well as in moments of complete surprise, mediate your presence to us now. Claim our highest thoughts, our best intentions, our dearest self-interest. Hold before us the cross of our Savior, that we may understand the mysteries and complexities of human existence and know that suffering is part of the nature of life. But show us also the Resurrection and remind us of the power to triumph over adversity and opposition. Enable us to put our faith in you and to live steadfastly from day to day, seeing an outcome we cannot presently reach and worshiping a Master we cannot presently touch. Reveal to us an inner ground of certainty in a world of change and upheaval. Let us walk as those who have heard a higher calling, and live as those who have been shaped for a higher destiny. Give strength to the weak and hope to the depressed. Touch with your healing hand the fevered brow and the tortured body. Soothe with your gentle voice the disturbed mind, the anxious heart, and the grieving soul. Open to us the benefits of your written Word and teach us to listen for the Voice that whispers from its pages. Keep in safety all who travel. Visit those in prison. Watch over the poor and homeless. And deliver us all from complacency and selfishness, that your kingdom may be known among us and your name honored in all we think or say or do, for Christ's sake. Amen.

97

O God, whose breath moves in everything that lives, and moves among us now, stirring us to new thoughts of what we may be and do in your love and freedom, help us to surrender to the luxury of your Spirit that we feel here and to the higher motivations you put within us. Help us to transcend the apathy and inertia that have bound us and open our lives to all the possibilities you have created for us. Let those who have lived with guilt and recrimination be released into the joy of forgiveness. Let those who have felt unworthy suddenly know their worthiness in your sight. Grant that those who have known too little of love and happy relationships may find themselves the objects of loving care and concern. Give healing to the sick and peace to the troubled. Let those who grieve release the persons or homes or prior mode of existence to which they have clung and find that they are content and even happy without them. In short, O God, enable us to see what green pastures you have led us to and to enjoy them now, knowing that it is in your love that you have given us life and opportunity and the energy to make a better world. Show us how we may be the servants of the poor and needy around us and how the kingdoms of this world may become the kingdom of our Christ. And let your name be glorified on earth as it is in heaven, through Jesus our Lord. Amen.

98

O God, whose generosity is so great that it always exceeds our ability to receive, with the result that our lives abound in blessings we have not noticed, we thank you for the world of grace and beauty around us: for shining sea and shadowed mountainside, for crowded city and gentle country, for the smell of flowers and the aura of books, for hard-crusted breads and soft ice cream, for fruit trees and vegetable stands and cattle farms, for schools and churches and banks and hospitals, for health and energy and naps and waking up, and for people—short people, tall people, fat people, thin people, loving people, cranky people, dull people, imaginative people, traditional people, innovative people, friendly people, shy people, people related to us, and people we shall never know. We could spend a lifetime looking at what you have made, Lord, and still not see it all. Teach us to behold mystery and miracle in the world and then to bow down in wonder before you. Let our eyes be open to the vast expanses of the universe and to the tiniest flower or snail in the garden. Above all, let us remember the special love you have for us as your people, sending your Spirit upon a man like us to be crucified for our salvation. Grant that this church may be a lively and imaginative response to the gospel of the kingdom and that we may be continually converted to the service of the poor, the home-less, and the misunderstood. Show us how to celebrate Christ's presence by loving one another and to witness to his lordship by being joyful and generous with all we have. Let the sharing of your Spirit bring happiness to all our guests this day, and to us as well. Send healing on those who are ill. Grant courage to those who face ordeals. Give peace to those who have been bereaved or burdened in any way. Speak to us through your Word and instruct our hearts in worship, that we may be lifted out of the ordinary framework of our lives and set in heavenly places to praise your name and see the world anew, for the sake of Christ our Lord. Amen.

99

Our Father, whose eternal design for our lives makes our own plans appear childish and limited, we open ourselves to you for your loving instruction. Show us how to yield to your way, how to grow beyond where we are now, how to find the power that reaches beyond all earthly barriers and limitations. Let our problems become opportunities for discovering your presence and your way around them. We hold before you all our friends in this sanctuary who are troubled in any way: those who are feeling tired and weak; those who can no longer cope with jobs or relationships or loneliness; those who need healing in their bodies; those who have had little time for faith and prayer; those whose lives have spun out of control; those who are agitated and restless; those who no longer know where to turn about anything. Hold them, dear God. Comfort them with your love. Inspire them with new hopes and dreams. Let their lives be different when they leave this place. Transform this church. Teach us to follow Jesus in his concern for others. Let our doors be truly open to all the wounded and under-valued people in society. Show us what can be accomplished through prayer and obedience. Remove our selfishness. Teach us to use our gifts. Bless us with a spirit of love and kindness. Nurture us in the understanding of the past and prepare us for the work of the future. Help us to sing and pray and worship like the angels in heaven. Glorify yourself in all our thoughts and actions. And when our work on earth is done, and we are ready to join that innumerable train of saints and servants always entering into their heavenly reward, let us quit this life with fondness and a kiss and enter the next one with a deep joy and satisfaction born of loving anticipation. For you are our God, and there is no greater guarantee of happiness. Through Jesus Christ our Savior. Amen.

100

O God, in whom are met all the issues of life and death, and who knows us and our frailties better than we know ourselves, we cast ourselves on your mercy and ask for your continued grace in our lives. We praise you for the little things that make our days so rich and meaningful: the love of a friend, the sight of a child sleeping, the memory of a good time, the sound of a particular voice, the appearance of a flower where yesterday there was none, the taste of good bread, the bouquet of a good wine, the thought of communion. Forgive us for days spent in not seeing, not hearing, not being open to the miracles that abound at our fingertips. Teach us to be sensitive: to know when a star falls, when a friend hurts, when the wind stirs, when the tides rise, when someone needs something we have in our possession. Show us, in our faith, how to be transparent so that others, looking at us, see you and know that all creation is one in your love. Guide our church into a new sense of what it means to be crucified for the world: to stop thinking about ourselves and start thinking about our neighbors; to stop trying to be great through "having" and start learning about being great through "serving." Stir our imaginations to see the new world the prophets saw, and the new world Jesus saw, and the new world our pilgrim ancestors saw, and let us recommit ourselves to that world in the present age—not a world of hurry and bustle and make-do and get-by, but a world of slowing down and listening and caring and sharing and celebrating the one true faith, revealed in a cross and an empty tomb. Embrace our visitors in your love. Lift the burdens of those whose hearts are heavy. Guide the lost back to the path. Touch with healing those who need it most. And help us to rejoice today in your Word and in the privilege of worship; for this is a special place, and a special hour, and we hope for a special encounter, through Jesus Christ our Lord. Amen.

101

O God, who is always present to us, yet known only when our hearts are quiet and we can feel you, teach us to be still and to know the mysteries that surround our lives. Save us from the madding crowd, the rushed sensibility, the agenda of anxiety, the day too filled for prayer and contemplation. Let the confidence and power that were in our Lord Jesus be also in us, that we may be directed by your Spirit and not by the world around us. Help us make the kind of commitment to you that will anchor our lives and prevent their being blown about by the winds of fashion or fancy. Have mercy on a world that seems to have lost its sense of the holy and lives frenetically by the production quota and the stock market. Show us how to be reverent again and to stand in awe before the sacred beauty of the created order. Let flowers and sunsets and wheat fields and foaming surf remind us of your eternity, and how closely you impinge on our daily existence. Save us from all that is cheap and glitzy and artificial, from every thought that debases, every appetite that devours, every ambition that blinds, every devotion that misleads our hearts. Let Christ be all in all. Let love for you and your world and your little ones consume our minds and souls. Let this church—let *every* church—become an island of caring and sanity and relationship in a sea where people are daily tempest-tossed and shipwrecked. Give healing to our sick; be doubly close to those in hospital and convalescent homes; grant easing of the heart to those who sorrow. Strengthen our children and young people for the temptations they must face and our elderly for the battles they must fight. Send enough light that we may walk our paths when darkness falls, and help us to trust you when there is no light at all. Be God in our midst and we shall proclaim you forever, Lord of Lords and King of Kings, world without end. Amen.

102

God of all beginnings and endings, who was old when the world began and will be fresh and young when it is ended, we return to you as to the fountain of all hope and energy, replenishing ourselves in your eternal being. We are grateful for life and its abundance: for food that tantalizes and satisfies, for work that fulfills, for sex that recreates, for rest that renews, for books that delight and instruct, for movies that probe and relax, for travel that regenerates, for love that empties, and for worship that carries us beyond ourselves. The world in which we live is rich and beautiful, varied and challenging. Forgive us for ever losing our taste for it or, by forgetting your presence in it, considering it redundant or difficult. As you have created the birds of the air and the beasts of the fields, create in us the appetite for adventure, the desire for wisdom, and the will to enjoy what you have given us. Teach us to live simply and elegantly, to walk humbly and sensitively, and to deal with life lovingly and flexibly. Help us to be like our Master, seeing eternity in a flower and building our lives on the solid rock. Let us believe in you so completely that nothing can deflect us from your service, and that there is no price we will not pay to be found faithful. Grant that we may remain always true to our ideals, helpful to other persons, and transparent to your will for our lives. Let those who are ill be healed, especially in spiritual ways, and let those who are lonely discover how far from alone they really are. Give guidance to our president and to all who lead their people in other nations, that this may be an era of growth in maturity and understanding for peace. Let your church be vigorously shaken and reordered, that it may once more follow in the way of him who was crucified for the sins of the world. And clothe yourself now in our worship and adoration, that your name may be glorified here and wherever we go, to the pleasure of all the saints and angels forever and ever. Amen.

103

We are gathered here out of many homes, O God, and many life experiences, yet common themes flow through our minds and hearts. Many of us have known conflict and struggle, and realize we have reached this hour only with your help and generosity. Some of us live with illness or physical disability and have often spoken your name out of weakness or despair. We have loved ones whose condition or behavior has made us anxious, and we have voiced our anxiety to you. Fears and uncertainties plague and paralyze us, and we have begged that these be taken away. We worry because we are alone, because no one cares, because we feel desperate or abandoned, and we have often prayed for our situations to be different. In other words, O God, we are all mindful of our finitude and inadequacy, our lostness and aloneness without you and others around us. It is the human condition of which we speak and the fact that we are always dependent on you for the most important things: for life itself, for love and companionship, and for strength and consolation and encouragement. Teach us to wait on you each day, in order that all our needs may be met in you and that we may learn not only to accept but also to celebrate our humanness. We are who we are and you are God, and that is a wonderful arrangement. Send healing on us and our loved ones and even on our enemies, if we have any, and bless our children and all prisoners and all who are in debt. And help us live in constant praise for the gospel of Christ, that in him you have shown us yourself and the grace that is able to overcome all our sins. For his name's sake. Amen.

104

A Pastoral Prayer for Summertime

There is something about this time of year that makes our hearts swell with rapture, O God. The summer heat, the dewy mornings and lingering dusks, children playing outdoors, the vacation gear, and the lure of holidays all combine to make us happy and carefree and expansive. But grant that we shall not forget or leave off the hard work of learning who we are and where our journeys should be taking us, or how we should be continuously grateful to you for the gift of our very existence. Nor let us neglect to remember our brothers and sisters throughout the world who may at this very moment be dying of illness or starvation or who are simply being overlooked, with no one to care for them or provide for their basic needs. Forgive us for not finding more creative ways of sharing what we have, or worse, for not even thinking of sharing. Use whatever means is necessary, O God, to make us sensitive, to imbue us with feelings for others, to give us a vision of the great importance of loving and providing for our brothers and sisters in the total family of the earth. Bless all the friends who have joined us for worship today. Give joy and strength to all who work in this community. Minister to the hurts and needs of everyone in our congregation and of all our loved ones, wherever they are. Teach us to sing and dance and rejoice in your kingdom as those who shall live forever, and we shall praise your name with unending delight. Through Christ our Lord. Amen.

105

O God, who is known in the glory of lakes and mountains and in starry nights and splendid sunsets and in the hum of great cities and the words of the prophets, but who is known best in the quietness of our own hearts when we listen for you to speak in wordless rhythms, we wait before you now in this special place, in the hush of these moments, and ask for your spirit to fall quietly upon us. Dispel our fears, ease the stress in our minds, remove all awkwardness, and, without audible words or overt signs, make a difference in our lives. Heal us of old hurts and wounds. Encourage us out of our despair. Be our companion in loneliness. Direct our paths. Enable us to love one another and to care about the world beyond us. Bless the visitors in our midst. Make this a good day for all nurses, doctors, police officers, firefighters, and others who must labor as we rest. Hear our particular prayers for *(Name)* and *(Name)* and *(Name)*, and others who are ill or grieving. Be with those who were recently married and make their lives rich with love and joy and simple companionship. And show us now how to undertake those quiet revolutions in our lives that will make all of life better, for ourselves and for others. Through Christ our Lord. Amen.

106

We confess, O God, that we do not often do extravagant things for others or for you. We learn at an early age to be guarded with our persons and possessions, hoarding them against a time when we might need them. And yet you are present in our lives every day, with a hundred opportunities to be kind and generous and loving: in the poor we know or meet along our way, in those who hunger for praise and recognition, in family members who need encouragement, in the shop clerks and waiters who serve us, in the dozens or even hundreds of nameless people we pass on the streets. Forgive us for withholding the gifts you have placed so abundantly in our hands, and teach us the joy of becoming free and open conduits of your blessing. Empower us to recognize your face in the faces of others, your handiwork wherever we look, and your Spirit surrounding our own spirits and inviting us to accept your wonderful hospitality. By the power in your Spirit, heal our sick, banish our grief, bless our visitors, and mold us into a heavenly fellowship worthy of your divine kingdom. For you are the God of all beauty and meaning and love, and we praise you through Christ our Lord. Amen.

107

We seldom pause in our busy lives, dear God, to think about how important the church is in the history of the world and in our own existence: what it has meant to the structuring of our faith and understanding, to the moral ordering of our universe, and to the modeling of such virtues as love, trust, service, and sacrifice. We thank you for the faith and obedience of the early followers of Christ, and for the devotion and imagination with which subsequent generations of the faithful have chosen to follow him. Grant that we in our time may likewise be faithful followers, denying ourselves and our more selfish impulses to promote the values and causes of Jesus and the apostles in a world that seldom understands or cares about them. Help us to believe even when the way is clouded by doubts and hardships, and to love others as Christ loved us, even to the point of suffering and death. Let this particular church, with its neighboring churches, be a beacon of light and hope to all who live in this community; and let our gifts, like those of the small boy who offered his few loaves and fishes to the Master, become a blessing to the multitudes. Smile upon our visitors today; give them rest and inspiration on their way. Comfort those who grieve, and bring healing to *(Name)* and *(Name)* and *(Name)* and others whose hurts or illnesses are on our hearts. Give us wisdom in the ordering of our lives and the disposition of our affairs. And help us live in peace and joy, praising you daily for the miracle of life itself. Through Jesus Christ our Lord. Amen.

108

Whenever we face a camera, O God, there is something about it that concentrates our minds and sends an instant message to our brains that we should look and behave our best. But we forget that you are always there, and there is no act of selfishness, no moment of ingratitude, no lapse into unkindness you do not see and remember forever. How then can we hope for forgiveness? How do we dare to ask for acceptance? And yet it was the message of Jesus, O God, that you have already forgiven and accepted and had mercy upon us. Surely this is the wonder of wonders and miracle of miracles! You have given us worth when we had none. You have loved us as thoughtless children wasting your gifts on the objects of our own pleasure and self-indulgence; and then, when we have spent all, you put rings on our fingers and robes on our backs and say, "Welcome home, child; you were lost but are found; you were dead but now you are alive."* Help us, dear God, not to squander so much of our lives in thoughtless and insensitive behavior, but to discover joy and peace and excitement in your presence before another day has passed, and to learn to live every hour in the welcoming embrace of your life-changing happiness. Then the camera will capture nothing but love and bliss and praise and ecstasy, world without end. Through Christ our Lord. Amen.

109

The world must have begun in silence, O God, and then moved to a crescendo of joyful music, with heavenly tympani crashing in rhythmic and glorious applause. Most of the important moments in our lives have likewise begun in silence: our conception in the womb, our innocent childhoods, falling in love, deciding upon our work, noticing you and how you have stood at every crucial turning of our life's journeys. We pray for something important to have its beginning now, as we wait before you: the resolution of some problem, the forgiveness of an enemy, a sense of love in our entire beings, commitment to a new way, the decision to seek and follow your will in our lives. Remove the impediments that have kept us from recognizing and responding to you. Give us peace in our inner beings. Let there be light where there was shadow, and joy where there was pain or depression. Help us to grieve and then let go of our grief. Teach us to listen to others and be patient with them. Show us how to love and celebrate our existence in the kind of world where we live. Restore fellowship where

---

* Luke 15:32, author's paraphrase.

it has been neglected. Heal the brokenness in our experiences and teach us to hope and trust and believe again. Give us a sense of eternity in this hour, that we may move out of silence into the joyful music of the future, and hear the wild drums beating out the magic tunes of heavenly visions. For you are God, and you can make it happen. Through Christ our Lord. Amen.

110
A Pastoral Prayer for a Lovely Day in Spring

In the beauty of a day like this, O God, our hearts are all but out of us. The tender leaves and shoots, the blooming flowers, the gentle breezes remind us of hope for the renewing of our own lives, and for the reenergizing of dreams we had all but abandoned, of love and peace, and gentleness in the whole creation. Here, in the community of faith, we ask your forgiveness for having forgotten your care and drifted away from your mercy. Restore us, we pray, to the deeper sanity we have known in you and rekindle in us a passion for righteousness. Show us how to act with justice, to love mercy, and to walk humbly with you. Give us victory over the addictions that have made us servants and not masters of our own way. Help us to think kindly of one another, and to speak gently, and to behave with compassion. Deal favorably with our infirmities, remembering especially our friends *(Name)* and *(Name)* and *(Name)*, and any others whom we may name in the privacy of our hearts. Comfort those who grieve. Cast a net of divine safety around our children and grandchildren. Ease the burdens of the elderly. Give leadership to our president and his cabinet, and to the Congress and the judicial system. And let this hour be one of wonderful healing and discovery for each of us, as the flowers bloom abundantly once more where we have experienced only barren and humdrum lives. Through Christ our Lord. Amen.

111

O God, whose way is so new and creative that we cannot be near you without being drawn into newer and more creative ways of living our own lives, give us the spirit of exploration and discovery that is commensurate with our coming here today. Show us the wonders that are waiting to be uncovered in the world, wonders some of us have come to regard as stale and repetitive. Take us by the hand, as we would take children, and lead us through doorways we have feared to enter and beyond barriers that have hindered our growth. Reveal miracles in our own behavior. Transform our attitudes, so that we live in excitement and expectation. Teach us to stand on tiptoe, listening for your voice and looking for the evidences of your presence. Help us to worship in a way that will help us notice you wherever we go and will make us servants of the general good. Bless our absent friends and loved ones; empower our visitors; heal those who need healing. Let the spirit of all life vibrate in our midst today and embolden us to become followers of your Christ, today and every day of our lives. For his name's sake. Amen.

112

When we are still, O God, life flows around us like a stream around a rock, and we have a sense of what it means to be centered in your eternity. Teach us to be still more often: when the day is hectic, when we are under attack, when others have lost their calm, when the news is bad and life appears to be deteriorating. In the stillness, we sense your presence and are healed. In the stillness, we know what is wrong in ourselves and can submit it to you for alteration. In the stillness, we become reoriented for living and can follow the right path once more. Take control of our lives again, O God. Become the guide, the driver, the pilot once more. Cleanse our hearts. Amend our attitudes. Restore our faith. Renew our energy. Use us to bless others around us and to renew our world. Remember our friends and loved ones who are ill or grieved or poorly used. Care for the poorest of the poor and the lowest of the low. Anoint our visitors with unexpected blessings. Enrich the lives of all families, especially single families struggling to be whole. And let our hearts rejoice in the beauty of everything around us without forgetting the pain and suffering of the world beyond us or even in the neighbor sitting beside us. Through Jesus Christ our Lord. Amen.

SEVEN

Communion Prayers

1

We offer praise and worship and thanksgiving to you, O God, for the gift of your Son Jesus Christ, whose death is commemorated in this bread and cup. Stir our hearts, we pray, to recall his suffering on the cross. Let the image of his lonely ordeal arouse our own passions, that we may take up again the earnest way of pilgrims and follow him obediently in our daily walk. Let us love and care and practice holiness, knowing that we shall eat and drink with him in the eternal kingdom. For his name's sake. Amen.

2

We eat and drink, O God, for joy and courage. Strengthen us now as we partake of this holy food, blessed by our memory of its tradition and by the presence of him who gives it. Let the troubled among us find peace. Give hope to any who are downhearted. Bind up the wounded and lift up the fallen. Open the eyes of those who cannot see. Let these fragments of bread and glasses of juice become the makings of a great feast in our lives, as Christ enters our hearts by them. Then we shall have joy in what is done and raise our voices in thanksgiving to you for your perfect gift of love and fellowship. For this is your table and we are your guests through Jesus Christ our Lord. Amen.

3

There is a special air at this table, O God, of tradition and memory, of depth and sacredness, of love and communion. We need such an air in our lives, which are prone to be lived with swiftness, thoughtlessness, and shallowness. It convicts us of sin and reminds us of our need for your forgiveness. Restore us, we pray, to fellowship with you and with one another, and to true integrity within ourselves. Let the health of this table overcome the disease of our hearts and minds and bodies. May Jesus' presence, which empowered the first disciples to become giants of the kingdom, enter our lives today, transforming them into lives of sanity, commitment, and generosity. May the bread and the cup become more than mere symbols on the table, may they become eternal food for our souls, whereby we grow into the gracious men and women you have designed us to be. Through Jesus Christ our Lord. Amen.

4

A Communion Prayer for Advent

O Lord, who came and dwelled in a stable so many years ago, come now and dwell in this bread and cup. Let us who have lived in darkness see you in the flickering light of candles, in the upturned faces of children, in the gnarled hands of the elderly as they reach for the elements. Feed our souls on holy food. We raise our prayers of glad thanksgiving for life and friends and family and food and church and for this table, set as a feasting board in our midst. Receive us here in our brokenness and need. Teach us new songs to sing and show us a new world to serve when we have eaten and drunk. Let mystery rise among us like smoke from burning wicks, and let joy settle over us like the soft lights of the Christmas tree. Speak to us through bread and cup and stir us to new devotion. For we long to be yours forever and ever. Amen.

5

A Communion Prayer for Christmas Eve

Our midwinters are never bleak, O Lord, when you are the Guest at our table. We greet you this Christmas eve with the excited air of those who have heard good news and once more remembered a Savior born in the little town of Bethlehem. There is a song in the air around us, and it is the song of redemption and hope. Angels we have heard on high, and kings we have seen coming to the stable. While shepherds watched their flocks by night, Messiah was born to gentle Mary, who laid her Child in a manger bare. It came upon the midnight clear, and songs rang out both far and near. It was joy to the world! Away in a manger, no crib for his bed, the Lord of all glory lay down his sweet head. "O come, O come, Emmanuel," we had cried for ages, "Come, thou long-expected Jesus." And in that silent night, holy night, the infant holy, infant lowly, was born, the brightest and best of the sons of the morning. We know that all mortal flesh should keep silence before the miracle, but we cannot help crying out, "Good Christian friends, rejoice!" and "God rest you merry, gentlemen!" Our Lord is here! He has come to save us! We praise his name forever! Amen.

6

This table is yours, O God; it is you who have set it before us. The bread is plentiful and the cup runs over. Both are full of meaning for our spirit-starved lives. As we eat the bread, we remember and give thanks for the One who said, "I am the bread of life. Whoever comes to me will never be hungry." As we drink from the cup, we recall and give thanks for the blood of the covenant which you swore with our fathers and mothers in the faith, that you would save us and make a great people of us. There is no worthiness in us that we should eat and drink from this table, but there is all worthiness in the Lamb that was slain. We are saved by his love. Therefore we eat and drink love here, and raise our voices in thanksgiving to you for the richest table in the world. Amen.

7

Some of us know, O God, how many strange things have happened around this table over the years and around other tables like it in other churches: people have seen Christ and decided to follow him; lives that were selfish and broken and full of fear have been turned around and given to him; whole congregations have suddenly been brought together in unity of spirit and dedicated to doing your will and changing the world for you. Let it be that kind of experience for us. Show us Christ in the bread and the cup. Let us remember his great suffering and his resurrection from the dead. Let us feel his presence here, warming our hearts and converting our desires. And then let us go out with the vision of all this burning in our minds, consuming us with joy and excitement, that your gospel of a new age and a new authority may be let loose in the world. Through him who died and was raised and now reigns with you, eternal in the heavens, world without end. Amen.

8

We are guests with Christ at this table, O God, whose worthiness to be here lies in him alone. Forgive our wayward spirits, which are always restless and at odds in the world and which often prevent the kind of daily experience of your presence we have professed to desire. Receive us as prodigal sons and daughters, and embrace us with loving acceptance according to the unlimitedness of your grace. Grant that we may have a strong and full impression of what it means to receive the body and blood of Jesus, and thus be bound to him in firmer ties of fellowship and service. Make of us one body in him, with each esteeming all others better than ourselves. And let our communion be with you and him and all the saints, that we may find our delight and strength in unity and not in separateness, which belonged to the betrayer Judas alone. Heal us in mind and soul and body, and anoint us with the sanctity of your Holy Spirit, that we may become your witnesses here and to the uttermost parts of the earth. In the name of Christ our Savior. Amen.

9

We gather at this table, O God, with adoration and confession and thanksgiving. We worship you for your greatness and your goodness, made known to us through your Word and your Son Jesus, and through the preaching of his followers down through the ages. We confess that we have not loved you above everything that is or breathes, and that we have not loved our neighbors, the miserable beggars in the streets and bazaars of Africa, the factory workers in Russia, or the idle rich of Newport and Hilton Head as much as we love ourselves. But we thank you for the redemption we experience through Christ Jesus—the forgiveness and renewal and restoration to purpose and commitment—that enables us to pick up our discipleship again, even months or years after laying it down, and follow once more in the way that leads to eternal life. Prepare our hearts for receiving this bread and cup, that the small things of life may lead to the larger and we may feel our hearts being filled with the presence and power and grace and love of our Savior, in whose beautiful name we pray. Amen.

EIGHT

Benedictions

1

May the Lord touch your lives with his wonder; the Lord open your eyes with his power; the Lord bless your coming and going with his watch-care; and the Lord lift your hearts with his love; now and forever. Amen.

2

Now may the grace of God, that floods the world we live in, find its way into the openings of your hearts, so that you may be swept out of yourselves this week and into the joy of the heavenly kingdom, in the name of the Father, Son, and Holy Spirit. Amen.

3

Now may God, who has begun a good work in us through Jesus Christ, bring it to completion in the days ahead for our eternal joy and salvation, in the name of the Father, Son, and Holy Spirit. Amen.

4

Now may God, who has called us to follow the Lord Jesus Christ, show us how to follow and make us obedient to the divine will forever and ever, in the name of the Creator, Child, and Holy Spirit. Amen.

5

Now may God, who has given us the world and all that is in it, give us the grace to live in it this week as humble servants, alert to all of life's possibilities and attuned to the heavenly kingdom, through Jesus Christ our Lord. Amen.

6

Now may the God of hearth and table bless you with plenty; may the Christ of love and compassion fill you with tenderness for all living things; may the Spirit of boldness and adventure enable you to overcome all obstacles in your own life; and to the Creator, Child, and Holy Spirit, one God, inseparable in nature and action, be glory forever and ever. Amen.

7

Now may God, who has brought us safely to this hour in the abundance of divine love and mercy, give you joy and peace and excitement in your daily lives by showing you the heavenly will for you, in the name of the Father, Son, and Holy Spirit. Amen.

8

May God, who has said Yes to us in Jesus Christ, help us to remember that affirmative word in all we do this week, in order that we may become yes-sayers to the world around us. In the name of the Father, Son, and Holy Spirit. YES!

9

Now may God, who has shown us a better life in Christ Jesus, give us that life in him this week, that we may share it with the world in grace and gladness of spirit. Amen.

10

Now may God, who has put in our hearts the love that cements all life together, bless you with the gift of gentleness and wonder of spirit this day and throughout this week, in the name of the Father, Son, and Holy Spirit. Amen.

11

May the God who created the world and all that is in it create in you this day a clean and happy heart, and give you love for all that the divine hand has fashioned, through Jesus Christ our Lord. Amen.

12

Now may God, whose love never lets us go, save, preserve, and keep you this day and forevermore, in the name of the Father, Son, and Holy Spirit. Amen.

13

Now may God, who is ever working to achieve the divine will in the world, bless you with the vision of that will and so draw you into it that your life can never be the same again, now and forever, in the name of the Father, Son, and Holy Spirit. Amen.

14

Now may the love and care that have kept us going until this moment be as personal to us as the Lord Jesus Christ and as near as his Spirit, in the name of the Father, Son, and Holy Ghost. Amen.

15

Now may the God who brought again from the dead our Lord Jesus, that great shepherd of the sheep, work in us to bring us all to new hope and life and peace, that the divine will may be perfectly fulfilled in us, this day and for all time to come. In the name of the Father, Son, and Holy Ghost. Amen.

16

Now may God, who speaks to us in many and wondrous ways, speak to us now and throughout this week in every tree that buds, in every face we see, and in every hand that reaches out and touches us. In the name of the Father, Son, and Holy Spirit. Amen.

17

May God, who brought the Israelites through the sea, Christ out of the tomb, and the church from martyrdom, bring you, who are loved beyond all words, through every trial and tribulation, every grief and burden, to the heavenly throne above, that you may sing with all the saints the song of joy forever and be gathered up with Christ to know the surpassing worth of all your faith. In the name of the Father, Son, and Holy Spirit. Amen.

18

Now may God, who has blessed us with freedom and joy and this beautiful land, make us truly thankful as we go forth from this place, and fill us with a spirit of love and generosity with which we may bless the whole world. In the name of the Father, Son, and Holy Spirit. Amen.

19

A Benediction for Advent

Now may the God who revealed the divine nature in a baby born in a stable reveal that nature to you this week in the simplest acts and least likely people in your lives. Through Jesus Christ our Lord. Amen.

20

A Benediction for Christmas

Go into the world with joy and peace and be men and women of goodwill. For it has pleased God to send a Son in our midst and give us a merry Christmas. Amen.

21

A Benediction for Christmas

Now may God, who brightened the night skies over Bethlehem and filled shepherds' hearts with mysteries and transformed a stable into a thing of immortal beauty, brighten your skies, fill your hearts with mystery, and transform your lives forever, in the name of the Father, and the Son, and the Holy Spirit. Amen.

22

Now may God, who is with us even in the valley of the shadow of death, give us peace in the divine will and joy in the divine presence, now and forevermore. In the name of the Father, Son, and Holy Spirit. Amen.

23

Now may our hearts be tuned to the very music of the heavens, that we may go our way singing and dancing, and thus attract others to the way of our God. In the name of the Father, Son, and Holy Spirit. Amen.

24

A Benediction for Easter

Now may the God who raised Christ Jesus from the dead, enabling him to call the name of Mary in the garden, raise you up with him from the deadness of your sin and give you life in the divine grace, both now and evermore. Amen.

25

Now may God, who has created us for fellowship with Christ and with each other, give us the courage to cross over every bridge that would bring us into the divine will and spirit, both now and evermore. In the name of the Father, Son, and Holy Ghost. Amen.

26

Now may God, who always makes time for us, help us make time for the divine Spirit, that our hearts may be ever filled with love and mercy and peace, through Jesus Christ our Lord. Amen.

27

Now may God, whose name is to be feared in all the earth, give you the grace to know the divine Spirit as a dear Parent, and to serve that Spirit this week with our Lord Jesus Christ. Amen.

28

May God, who has gone before our community in fire and cloud, go before us now in peace and joy, preparing the hearts of all people to receive the witness of our good-will, in the name of the Father, Son, and Holy Spirit. Amen.

29

Now may God, who gives us life and love, nourish us with the sunlight of divine presence, that we may grow in all spiritual graces, through Jesus Christ our Lord. Amen.

30

Now may God, who made the world and all that is in it, show us how to live in peace wherever we go and how to love one another in tender mercy, in the name of the Father, Son, and Holy Spirit. Amen.

31

Now may God, who has given us this day in which to rejoice and be glad, help us to have more love for Christ and for the least of his children, in the name of the Creator, Child, and Mothering Spirit. Amen.

32

Now may the God we have met in the holiness of this hour go before us into the world and prepare places of service for us, that we may share with others the love and joy we have felt here, in the name of the Father, Son, and Holy Spirit. Amen.

33

Now may God, who calls us from where we are and stands at the end of our journey, be with each of us at every step of the way, in the name of the Father, Son, and Holy Spirit. Amen.

34

Now may God send a blessed spirit with us wherever we go and remind us always of the divine love and generosity in our lives, that we in turn may freely bless the world and all who live in it. In the name of the Father, Son, and Holy Spirit. Amen.

35

Now may God, who has made the world and filled it with beauty, give you eyes to see the mysteries and miracles around you and make your hearts rejoice this day and evermore. In the name of the Father, Son, and Holy Spirit. Amen.

36

May you leave this place feeling strongly connected to God, who has led his people in all the ages, in order that he may lead you in joy today and forever. In the name of the Father, Son, and Holy Spirit. Amen.

37

Now may God smile upon you this day with eternal love and favor, and may you know it, so that you are encouraged to love your life and to celebrate it, even when there is pain and difficulty. In the name of the Father, Son, and Holy Ghost. Amen.

38

May the Spirit of God come upon you like the morning dew and explode in your hearts like fireworks on the Fourth of July, filling you with excitement and gladness every day that you live, in the name of the Father, Son, and Holy Spirit. Amen.

39

May the God of this bright and beautiful world make your lives bright and beautiful this day and forever, in the name of the Father, Son, and Holy Spirit. Amen.

40

Now may God, who has loved us with such an incredible faithfulness, send us forth to be faithful lovers of his world and of all those who dwell in it. In the name of the Father, Son, and Holy Spirit. Amen.

41

May you be kept always in the Father's love, in the Son's service, and in the Spirit's power, this day and forevermore. Amen.

42

May the God of eternal springtime make flowers spring up in your hearts and souls this day and every day, world without end. In the name of the Father, Son, and Holy Spirit. Amen.

43

May God give us the ability to see the divine glory in everything that is and everyone we meet, so that we may revel in the divine presence every day of our lives. In the name of the Father, Son, and Holy Spirit. Amen.

44

May God give you the joy of divine fellowship and the hope of everlasting life in Christ, that your days may be inexpressibly full, in the name of the Father, Son, and Holy Spirit. Amen.

45

Go now in the realization that God's arms are always around you and that there is no more important thing you can do this day than discover the great difference this makes in everything! In the name of the Father, Son, and Holy Spirit. Amen.

46

Now may the sweet, sweet spirit of God follow you wherever you go, this day and forever, and may it infect everyone you meet, in the name of the Father, Son, and Holy Spirit. Amen.

47

May God give you a spirit of love and happiness this day that will change your life forever, and then open the windows of your soul so that you can share it with the whole world. In the name of the Father, Son, and Holy Spirit. Amen.

48

Now may God, who has brought us together again in joy and fellowship, attend our going out with his love and care, that we may be a blessing to everyone we meet, today and all this week. Amen.

49

Let the peace that is in our hearts and minds through our Lord Jesus Christ become the peace of the whole, wide world, and may we all be caught up in his service today and forever. In the name of the Father, Son, and Holy Spirit. Amen.

50

Now may God, who is faithful to us in every situation, make us strong to do his will and compassionate to care for all his little ones. In the name of the Father, Son, and Holy Spirit. Amen.

51

May the God who has filled our world with evidences of the divine presence open our eyes to see and our ears to hear, that we may live vividly and joyfully, in the name of the Father, Son, and Holy Spirit. Amen.

52

May you look in the mirror this week and smile at the face God has given you, and may you one day look into the face of God and see your own face and know how much God loves you. In the name of the Father, Son, and Holy Spirit. Amen.

A Psalm

Offered Following the Tragic Events of
September 11, 2001

Into the innocence and gaiety of our everyday lives
flew four airplanes,
like the four horsemen of the Apocalypse,
each burdened with hate and fury and vengeance.
Our twin towers of hope and trust
cascaded to the ground
in vast piles
of dust and death and debris.

Where were you, O God,
when it happened?
Did it make you think
of all that suffering and destruction
produced by your Son's coming into the world,
beginning with the nails driven into his hands on the cross
and the slaughter of multitudes
of noble and innocent people
across the ages?

Where were you, O God,
when mothers and fathers and sons and daughters
in those fragile flying machines
exploded into walls of glass and girders of steel?
Where were you
when poor souls leapt
from the tops of flaming buildings
into air filled with smoke
and plunged 32 feet per second per second
onto the unforgiving surfaces of cars and concrete below?

Where are you now, O God,
as relatives stand numbly on street corners,
wearing the photographs of their loved ones
who cannot be found,
and rescue workers tear desperately
at impossible heaps of stone and steel,
weeping in the rain for victims they know are there
but they cannot reach?

Where are you now, O God,
when a nation mourns
for its lost children
and little children themselves
are numb with shock and grief
because their world of happiness and security
has been breached by four planes,
the horsemen of the Apocalypse?

Surely you are as hurt as we are, O God,
for you have always been a compassionate and caring God,
whose living faithfulness has pursued us all of our lives,
even when we were paying no attention to you
because there were too many other things on our minds
and our hearts were full of ourselves.

Could it be that
that is why we have such trouble now
understanding the horror of these past few days
and trying to make sense
of a loving God who permits such tragedies?

If only we had been closer to you,
dwelling in hourly communion with your spirit,
we might have felt less impact when the horsemen struck,
for you have been dealing with these things
since the beginning of time

and are more immune to shock and surprise.
You have wept in your own way
over the inhumanity of man to man
and the acts of treachery and perfidy
that have often shattered friendships
and destroyed communities.
And on the cross of Calvary
you felt the nails go in
with agonizing disbelief
that love itself, the final offering,
could be dismissed so easily
by hearts as hard
as flint.

Yet out of the death and betrayal of the cross, O God,
you have fashioned new instruments of hope and trust
and taught us to find comfort
in a cup of wine and a loaf of bread,
as if a body broken for us
might one day symbolize all joy
and all redemption,
a world finally fashioned
into the kingdom of our God,
and an everlasting community of love.

Where are you now, O God?
You are there, in the twisted steel and rubble,
in the solidarity of rescue workers and firefighters and
    police,
in the millions of people hoping, praying,
for just one more person to be saved.
And you are here in this very place,
with us in our shock and grief,
feeling the pain of our pain
and the agony of our distress.
And you are in thousands of places

where people have gathered to pray and worship,
trying to find their way once more
through the maze of wounded feelings
to a place where they can breathe again.
You are there, and you are here,
and in all these places
you are working to bring good out of evil
and shining redemption from grim destruction.

In all these places
you are saying to us,
"Be still in your heart, my child,
and know that I am God.
I have not abandoned you,
nor will I ever do so.
For I have loved you from the beginning of time,
and I have prepared a place for you,
that where I am you may always be.
I know things do not look good now,
and your heart is deeply troubled,
but wait until morning, when the storms are past,
and you will find your hope again,
and your trust,
and you will realize, my child,
that I have never left you,
even in the darkest times.
And you will know,
with the rising of the sun,
that I have not left you now."